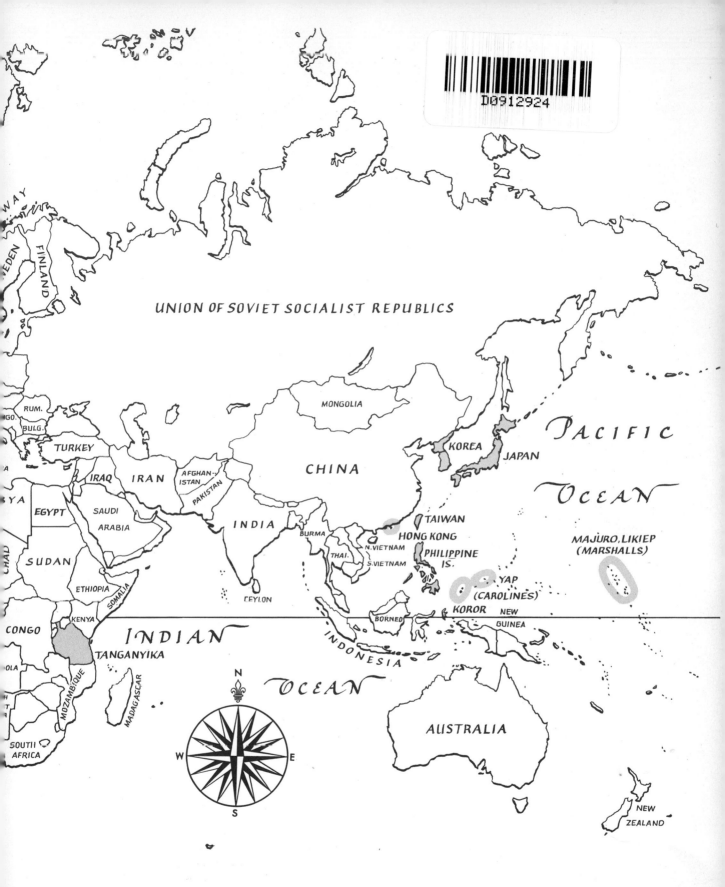

UNION OF SOVIET SOCIALIST REPUBLICS

PACIFIC

OCEAN

MONGOLIA

CHINA

KOREA

JAPAN

RUM.

BULG.

TURKEY

IRAQ

IRAN

AFGHAN-
ISTAN

PAKISTAN

INDIA

TAIWAN

HONG KONG

MAJURO, LIKIEP
(MARSHALLS)

EGYPT

SAUDI
ARABIA

BURMA

THAI.

N.VIETNAM

S.VIETNAM

PHILIPPINE
IS.

YAP
(CAROLINES)

SUDAN

CEYLON

KOROR

NEW
GUINEA

ETHIOPIA

SOMALIA

CONGO

KENYA

INDIAN

BORNEO

INDONESIA

OLA

TANGANYIKA

MOZAMBIQUE

MADAGASCAR

OCEAN

SOUTH
AFRICA

N

W   E

S

AUSTRALIA

NEW
ZEALAND

palacios

MARYKNOLL SISTERS

A PICTORIAL HISTORY

MARYKNOLL SISTERS

A PICTORIAL HISTORY

BY *Sister Mary Francis Louise*

E. P. DUTTON & COMPANY, *Inc.*

NEW YORK   1 9 6 2

TO OUR LADY

CONTENTS

MARYKNOLL SISTERS

A PICTORIAL HISTORY

I

New Joy / 1906 *to* 1920

MARY JOSEPHINE ROGERS hurried down the rickety old stairs from the Boston Propagation of the Faith office, clutching a cumbersome bundle of old albums and photographs in her arms, and experiencing a strange new joy in her heart. She was twenty-four years old, and had found her life's work. She did not know then its magnitude, nor did she suspect that as Mother Mary Joseph it would make her the Foundress of America's first Catholic missionary Sisterhood. She knew only that she had found the work she loved.

When she got home that raw December evening in 1906, she appropriated the family bathtub and began her first mission work—ungluing the numerous photographs from the album pages and backings, so that they could be used in a new mission magazine, *The Field Afar*. As she went about this work, her thoughts wove back and forth across the events of the past few weeks.

It had really begun when Miss Hanscomb asked her to tea. Miss Rogers, newly graduated from Smith College, was now a Fellow in Zoology there. Her parents, Abraham and Mary Josephine Rogers, were proud of the achievement of their first daughter, Mary, known to the family as Molly, one of eight children. She had gone

through Smith, after graduating from the public schools of Jamaica Plain, where the Rogers' home was, and on graduation the college offered her the fellowship. Miss Elizabeth Hanscomb was one of Smith's senior teachers, and faculty adviser to all religious clubs. In this capacity, and conscious of Miss Rogers' remarkable qualities of leadership, Miss Hanscomb's invitation to tea was part of her plan to encourage Molly to form a study club of Catholic students.

"Why don't you start a little group for the Catholic students?" Miss Hanscomb suggested as she poured the tea. "Perhaps a Bible-study club."

Molly smiled at this faithful Protestant, and was warmed by her generous spirit. "I'm not sure I'm qualified for that," she replied, "but I'm impressed with the work the Protestant students do for their missions."

"Well, then, my dear," Miss Hanscomb urged, "start a mission club." And that's just what Molly did.

There is in the Church an organization called the Society for the Propagation of the Faith, with a director in each diocese. Although America was then still considered a territory to which missioners were sent, the Diocese of Boston had a Propagation Director, a young priest, Father James Anthony Walsh, who together with Father Thomas Frederick Price would cofound the American mission society of priests—the Maryknoll Fathers. Miss Rogers was referred to Father Walsh by her pastor. She visited his office to get further information with which to foster interest in her prospective club.

"I found him," Mother Mary Joseph wrote many years later, "at his headquarters on Union Park Street, opposite the Cathedral. Such a surprising ready-to-tumble-down place it was! Narrow, rickety stairs and a dark hall led to the 'rookery,' as he called his office, and it was with a sense of relief that I saw in the sun's revealing light a room lined with books, here and there on the wall bright splotches of color, a large desk, on the table beside it, a globe, and at the desk, smiling a welcome, the Director himself."

Strangely enough, both of these people had an intuition that their most important work was about to begin. When he was assigned to the position of Director of Propagation of the Faith, Father Walsh knew in his heart he would spend the rest of his life in foreign-mission work of one kind or another. Writing later on this first meeting, Miss Rogers, as Mother Mary Joseph, says: "I was unknown to him, seeking information on foreign missions, but in my soul there was already lighted a spark of apostolic fire that awaited the gentle breath of heaven to fan it into a living flame. He was to be that breath. I who had gone in as a stranger that day, left him, as hundreds of others have left him, with a warm sense of kinship and a quickened consciousness of joyful obligation to others, the fulfillment of which would have real value for me only if motivated by a love of souls in Christ."

The mission club was begun, but at the same time a fuller interest was born in Miss Rogers' heart. For the next six years she gave whatever she had of leisure time to fostering the cause of the Catholic mission by whatever means she could. With America still counted as a mission land, the principal work was to awaken Ameri-

cans to their privilege of serving Christ's needs elsewhere. On October 4, 1906, Father Walsh, together with Father James F. Stanton and Father John I. Lane of Boston, and Sulpician Father Joseph Brunneau, had begun a bimonthly review of mission work called *The Field Afar*. A great deal of Miss Rogers' mission work in the six years that followed was preparing copy for this publication, beginning with her first project of ungluing the photographs.

The first issue of *The Field Afar* came out in January, 1907. Father Walsh was going over the initial galleys when Mary Josephine Rogers first visited his office in December, 1906. He showed them to her and asked her what she thought of the idea of something more alive to replace the Annals of the Propagation, a translation of letters from missioners through Rome into various languages, which was very dull and very old.

To make the missions known to Catholic America was Father Walsh's immediate apostolate, for he knew that a willing response would come if Americans knew the needs. But the need for an American seminary for missioners grew apace. As far back as 1907, in his annual report to the Society for the Propagation of the Faith, he wrote: "While the missionary spirit which is developing in the Archdiocese must inevitably produce vocations for foreign lands, this call has not yet manifested itself clearly in any individual. Yet no fewer than nine young men and women have seriously approached the director on this sacred subject."

Where were these vocations to be fulfilled? The need grew and grew until in God's loving care another meeting occurred. In September, 1910, at the Eucharistic Congress in Montreal, Father Walsh met Father Thomas Frederick Price of North Carolina with whom he had corresponded for many years. After their meeting in the lounge of a Montreal hotel, the Catholic Foreign Mission Society began to come into reality. Through their united and persevering efforts, and the wholehearted cooperation of the American hierarchy, these two priests succeeded

Mary Josephine Rogers, taken on September 6, 1912, two days before she came to Maryknoll.

by June 29, 1911, in obtaining the permission of the Holy Father, St. Pius X, to open a seminary to train Americans for the missionary priesthood.

They returned from Rome and began at once to look for a place to call home, for students, and for the means to support the new work. They decided upon New York as a most central location, and in September, 1911, established headquarters at Hawthorne, New York, with the help of the Dominican Fathers. The need to transfer *The Field Afar* operation to the same locality was quickly evident, and when this was done, three young women who had been doing volunteer work for the publication in Boston volunteered to come to New York and help the new mission society in whatever way they could.

They arrived in Hawthorne on January 6, 1912, the feast of the manifestation of Christ to the Gentiles. This is the date the Sisters celebrate as their real beginning. The young women, called the "secretaries," were Mary Louise Wholean, a graduate of Wellesley College; Sara Sullivan, who had been on the dean's office staff at Harvard Medical School; and Mary Augustine Dwyer, an experienced office worker. Forty-three years later, Sister Mary Teresa, formerly Sara Sullivan, gave an account of their arrival.

"On the morning of January 6th, we took the train for Hawthorne. We were three girls, Mary Wholean, Mary Dwyer and myself, and none of us knew each other.

"We had met at the New York Cenacle where Father Walsh suggested we spend a few days on retreat before coming. This we did, and also a little shopping, and then we got the train. Father Walsh met us at the station and took us to the house he had rented for us. He and his friend, Father Lane, stayed to help us, as well as a neighbor's boy Father Walsh had hired for the day. The boy reminded us that tomorrow would be Sunday and the stores would be closed. We had forgotten to get bread with the rest of the groceries and he went off to get it for us.

"Later, while we busied ourselves getting supper, Father Lane was still opening packing cases

and Father Walsh was putting up pictures around the house to make it more home-like. As they left that evening, Father Walsh waved his hand vaguely over my shoulder and said, 'The church is over there.'

"The next morning the world was white with snow. We could see neither path nor road, but started off in the direction of the wave. Eventually we came to a large building with a cupola, which I thought must be the church, though the front and side doors were still locked. Finally I said, 'Let's look in the window.' One peep was enough; it was the village fire station.

"We trudged on through the snow until we came to a fairly large house. One of the doors stood wide open and there were a couple of chairs outside, with a box on each holding a few dimes. I knew then we had reached the Catholic Church."

Very shortly thereafter, Nora Shea, who had been Father Walsh's secretary at the Boston Propagation Office, joined the group. They had more than enough to do. In addition to the editorial and clerical work, they had to haul water from a somewhat distant well, and cook over a wood stove, in an unheated, candlelit house. The well proved to be the home of several snakes, so another one, even farther away, became their source of water, until Mother Alphonsa Lathrop, of the Cancer Home, learned of their plight and supplied them with a tub of fresh water daily.

When September came, the seminary opened and three students arrived. They were Francis X. Ford, later Bishop of Kaying, China, who died in a Communist prison; James Edward Walsh, second Father General of the Society, and Bishop of Kongmoon, presently imprisoned by the Communists in Shanghai; and William F. O'Shea, later Bishop of Pyeng Yang, Korea, who died of a heart attack in 1945.

Mary Rogers longed with all her heart to be with the "secretaries," but family obligations kept her in Boston until September. However, on Our Lady's birthday, September 8th, she too came to Hawthorne, bringing with her Margaret

Shea, the newest volunteer, only seventeen years old.

"For some time I had been trying to get into a convent," explained Sister Mary Gemma, the Margaret Shea of many years before. "My confessor had done everything in his power to help me. He'd given me four or five letters of introduction to various convents, but after visiting them I would come back and tell him that although I thought the Sisters were very nice indeed and their work was wonderful and all that, still, for some reason or other, I did not feel attracted to that particular congregation. Finally my confessor laughed, and said, 'Well, I guess there's nothing to do but make an order to suit you.'

"Shortly after that, Father called me and said that Father Walsh, whom he had known as Director of the Society for the Propagation of the Faith in Boston, was starting a new seminary. Father Walsh had been in town that day and had visited him. Father Walsh said he had four women in the offices to work as secretaries and to help in this enterprise, and he was now looking for some other young people who would also be willing to go. 'What do you think of this?' Father asked me. Immediately the proposal appealed to me; I said I would love to go, and asked what I should do about it.

"I called Father Walsh the next morning, but unfortunately he was unable to see me since he was leaving for New York that day. But he gave me the address of Molly Rogers. Her home was not very far from where I was living, so the following day I went over to see Molly. She already knew about me, since Father Walsh had told her I was coming, and she gave me a very warm welcome. The only thing she said was that I looked very young to know my own mind. But then she asked: 'Are you free to go? You haven't any obligations here?' I was free, and we finally decided to leave for New York on the 8th of September."

"I found everything," Mother Mary Joseph wrote later, "astir over two great events: the incoming of the first group of seminarians and the impending move to the recently bought property on Sunset Hill above Ossining—the real Maryknoll."

The property consisted of fifty-two acres of farmland with several colonial-style houses, one of which was assigned to the young women. On September 18th the priests and students moved there, seven of them crowded into a carriage meant for four, clinging to the oil lamps that would provide light in their new home. The secretaries followed on October 15th, the feast of St. Teresa of Avila, after whom they were then named Teresians, and their house, St. Teresa's Lodge.

"The woman's part," Molly Rogers wrote, "was quite naturally ours. While the seminarians made their studies or worked with the Brothers in house and field, we found joy in serving them as cook, laundress, seamstress and secretary. I like to recall that mine was the privilege of being the first of our Sisters to cook for the Seminary. Frightened by the isolation of the new Maryknoll, the cook fled during the night, leaving a bewildered 'father' of a cookless family. He called on us for help as soon as the desertion was realized."

Miss Rogers was the favorite cook of the seminarians, although not of the "father" of the family who "fired" her as soon as he could for making too many toothsome desserts for his students and undermining the family budget. However, cooks came and went rapidly, and with each disappearance the students looked forward to another few happy days of Miss Rogers' delicious cuisine. In the end the secretaries added the kitchen duties to their already heavy office work.

Very shortly they added handling the laundry to their burgeoning duties, and there was work and to spare. The amount and hazards of this work are described by a student seminarian of those days who was later to become Bishop Raymond A. Lane, third Superior General of the Maryknoll Fathers:

Photographs taken on the Maryknoll Seminary's
farm in 1914 show Sister Teresa feeding the
horses and (below) Sister Mary Joseph (later
Mother) taking care of the calves.

The first home of the secretaries in Hawthorne, New York, to which they came on January 6, 1912.

The first seven who came to help Father James A. Walsh with his new mission work, as they appeared in 1912. Seated, left to right: Mary Wholean became Sister Mary Xavier; Anna Towle became Sister Anna Maria; Mary Josephine Rogers became Mother Mary Joseph; Sara Sullivan became Sister Teresa. Standing, left to right: Mary Dwyer, who did not remain with the group; Nora Shea became Sister Theophane; Margaret Shea (no relation to Nora), now Sister Gemma in Japan.

*On St. Teresa's day, October 15, 1912, the pio-
neer seven moved into an old farmhouse on the
Sunset Hill compound in Ossining and named
their new home St. Teresa's.*

"The secretaries' home was St. Teresa's. As you entered the old house there was a big room at your right. Mail desks, filing cabinets, bookkeeping equipment filled this room. Here you found everything connected with the editing and publishing of a magazine, including the address files and benches for mailing. How did all that office furniture, with incoming mail and out-going magazines, fit in that small space and still leave room for the Teresians to move about? I don't know: it's a mystery.

"I can see them now, that first group on Monday mornings, turning out the laundry in a small basement room filled with steam. It's another mystery how in the world they ever fitted into that tiny cubby hole, which was already over-crowded with tubs. Again, Miss Rogers was in the midst of it, up to her collar in suds."

The job Miss Rogers kept for herself was washing a tubful of the seminarians' socks by hand. One of the Sisters later described the operation: "She took the tub, put it on the table and went through it. How often the water ran muddy, and sometimes for lack of water we couldn't do anything to rinse the wash."

Among themselves the secretaries had begun to strive for a religious life. Mary Dwyer did not feel this was her vocation, but so as not to deter the others from their goal, she withdrew. Father Walsh began to look for a Congregation of Sisters that could give the group the training for religious life that the Church requires.

Meanwhile Mary Josephine Rogers was naturally accepted by the group, and in fact assigned by Father Walsh to lead them. They began to center their life on Mass, meditation, and silence. On May 5, 1913, they decided to wear a simple cotton uniform. Miss Rogers had a dress they all liked. It was gray chambray with a jabot, and became the basis of the Community's habit. They still called one another by their own names prefixed by Mary—Mary Nora, Mary Louise, and Miss Rogers became Mary Joseph.

In 1914 Cardinal Farley of New York gave the group permission to be called a Pious Society of Women. But the first efforts to establish a religious congregation met with many heart-breaking setbacks. Holy Mother Church requires that any new organization that wishes to take public vows receive formal training in the responsibilities of religious life from a previously established Congregation of Sisters. None of the pioneer women who came to Maryknoll had had formal training as Religious, although each had aspirations for spiritual growth.

Efforts to comply with the directions of the Church began with arrangements to have the Franciscan Missionaries of Mary come to train the group. The Sisters so assigned were instead re-directed to their missions in Africa. In the meantime, the Teresians decided to say daily the Little Office of the Blessed Virgin to give expression to their growing spirit of Community.

Then on September 15, 1914, three Immaculate Heart Sisters (Sisters Stanislaus, Gerard, and Domitilla) from Scranton arrived, and their formal religious training began. The length of such training differs from one Community to another, but the basic requirement is a period of postulancy followed by a full year of novitiate. Under the direction of these Sisters, the Teresians began to wear postulants' dress in February of 1915. On January 6, 1916, they voted on affiliation with the Carmelites, Franciscans, or Dominicans, and chose the Dominicans. But less than a month later they learned that their postulancy and novitiate with the Immaculate Heart Sisters were not valid, since the required preliminary approval had not been secured from the Holy See. The Immaculate Heart Sisters, unable to help them further, returned to Scranton, and the work had to be begun again. In spite of these setbacks the Teresians continued to draw women to their vocation, though at that time few girls coming to Maryknoll received encouragement from family, friends, or pastor. "Why not go to an established Community?" was the usual advice, but the missionary vocation is a gift of itself, and America's

young daughters came to Maryknoll despite opposition. They began then to use religious names. Miss Rogers was chosen directress, and became Sister Mary Joseph; Mary Wholean became Sister Mary Xavier; Sara Sullivan, Sister Teresa; Nora Shea, Sister Theophane; Margaret Shea, the youngest, became Sister Gemma; and Anna Towle, Sister Anna Maria.

The Teresians formally petitioned Rome for the right to open a novitiate, and at the same time received a promise from Mother Samuel of the Sinsinawa Dominicans of Wisconsin to send them a novice mistress when the novitiate was opened. Two months later the petition was returned. It had been directed to the wrong office in Rome. The disappointments kept piling on.

In February, 1917, Sister Mary Xavier died, the first death in the Maryknoll family. Father Walsh offered the Requiem Mass, but afterward in the sacristy he broke down and sobbed for

The Tin Lizzie, politely known as "Elizabeth" (and chauffeured, tradition says, by Frank Ford who later became Bishop of Kaying, China, and died in a Communist prison), was their means of going on picnics on special occasions, such as this outing at Far Rockaway on St. Teresa's Day, 1915. The man walking around the front is Father James A. Walsh, co-founder of Maryknoll.

grief. The Teresians determined to deepen their religious life to cope with these hardships. They received a silver Chi-Rho ring to wear as a symbol of fidelity. Father Walsh appointed superiors for a year: Sister Mary Joseph, superior; Sister Mary Teresa, assistant superior; Sisters Catherine, Gemma, and Magdalen, councilors; Sister Theophane, treasurer.

The year 1918 began with little better hope. The country was at war, and times were hard for all. Their greatest joy that year, laced with the grief of separation, was the Fathers' first mission departure. Led by Father Price, Fathers Ford, J. E. Walsh, and Bernard Meyer departed for China. The Sisters prepared a sumptuous dinner, and afterward were in the kitchen cleaning up. Father Price, at the front door, stopped and said, "Where are the Sisters?" He wouldn't take another step until all came to say goodbye and see them off. It was the last time they saw

July 4, 1916—the growing "society of pious women" had their picture taken. They numbered fifteen, and looked forward hopefully to becoming Sisters.

their Father "Bernadette"—so named for his beloved St. Bernadette—for he died on the mission in September, 1919.

Sister Mary Joseph, as superior of the Community, was a practical idealist, and undaunted by difficulties. She had an ideal for her Sisters that she expressed with succinct richness years later. The spirit to which she gave form came from her own generous heart, the wisdom of Father Superior (Walsh), and the apostolic zeal of an ardent Spaniard, who lived centuries before — the friar-preacher St. Dominic.

Sister was always first, more by example than by words, in the virtues she recommended to others. She loved good sense. When she found Sister Gemma, her littlest daughter, about to scrub the kitchen floor late one evening after a long day in the laundry, she remonstrated: "Now, that can be left for some other time. You go to bed, dear." Sister Gemma went gratefully, but later began to worry that Sister Mary Joseph would do the floor herself. However, she was reassured when she heard Sister coming upstairs quite shortly after. Nevertheless, next morning, Sister Gemma found a sparkling kitchen floor. "The angels did it, no doubt," said Sister Mary Joseph with a quick smile. Much later Sister Gemma found that Sister Mary Joseph had swabbed the floor in less than half an hour in her own inimitable style. She had boiled a pail of soap scraps and flooded the greasy floor with it. After spreading the hot soap all around, she rinsed it with several more pails of clear boiling water and swept it out over the back porch.

Sister Mary Joseph somehow managed to make good common sense part of her virtue. One night Sister Gemma couldn't sleep; something dreadful was hanging over the Community. (Years later, Sister couldn't even remember what the impending doom was, but at the time it seemed fearfully distressing.) As Sister tossed around in bed, she thought that poor Sister Mary Joseph must be in even worse straits. She said to herself: "I'll go in and comfort her. At least the two of us will have each other." But when she slipped into Sister's room, she found her sound asleep, enjoying a good night's rest. "Well, if she isn't worried, why should I be?" thought Sister Gemma, and back to her room she went, to sleep blissfully through the rest of the night.

Sister Mary Joseph was fond of fun. When she was Mother General, she patiently allowed Father Cotta, a beloved China missioner who became the Sisters' chaplain, to pose her at a variety of places on the porches and at the windows of the convent, so that he could produce a trick photograph showing seven Mother Mary Josephs at once.

Newcomers kept arriving, and they came from every American background: from deeply religious families and from those who never prayed at all; working-girls arrived with those just returning from a last trip to Europe; professional women joined high-school graduates— and they had all found the same vocation—Love.

Many years later one of these early comers wrote of her own experience: "Mine was a happy home, with the most devoted parents. They were rich in this world's goods, but poor in the things that matter for eternity. Father came from an old Catholic family, but he practically lost his Faith while completing his education in Europe. Mother was a convert, and not well instructed. They were married in the Church, but neither practiced his religion. We children were taught no prayers, and at school religion was given the last consideration.

"At about eleven I was sent to a nearby convent school to prepare for First Communion and Confirmation. Mother scarcely understood the life of nuns, and warned me not to let them kiss me for they might have TB and their black habits were unhygienic! There was nothing in my life or education to foster a religious vocation. For my part, I thoroughly enjoyed all the world had to offer. We traveled extensively, and lived abroad for several years. I studied art and music, played tennis and golf, and rode. I loved pretty clothes, and my every wish was gratified by my father.

"Strange to relate, I cannot recall a time when, in the depths of my heart, I did not *know* that God called me. I knew, also, that I should and would follow Him. Still I took no steps to inquire when or where. Meanwhile, like most girls in my station of life, I had many opportunities to marry, but I was twenty-five before I faced and solved my problem.

"It started when my sister gave me St. Teresa's autobiography to read. Following this I discovered the works of Father Frederick Faber. My delight in my first missal and the thrill of following the inspired prayers of the Mass, I will never forget. Daily Mass became the great act of my life, which I hid at home with difficulty. My parents were far from wishing a daughter of theirs to enter the convent.

"I was given the names of several Communities with whom I became acquainted, but I did not feel a particular attraction toward any. I was left with an impression of too much external formalism, and then the habits were so impractical! The great Teresa would have conformed to the times, thought I!

"About this time I had the good fortune to meet Father James Anthony Walsh, and he invited me to Maryknoll to meet the 'Teresians.' A friend offered to take me to Maryknoll for a weekend, cautioning me to dress plainly and not to expect butter or cake, for the 'Teresians' were very poor. To our amusement, both butter and cake appeared on the table that first evening.

"This small group, only the nucleus of a religious Community at the time, crystallized my religious vocation. I found tangible poverty with an irresistible appeal, making me think of the holy home of Nazareth. I found the spirit of Maryknoll: an indefinable radiation of loving, joyous dedication. I found, or rather glimpsed, in Sister Mary Joseph, a rare combination of most lovable natural gifts with a spirituality flowing fresh and deep from the fountains of the Holy Spirit.

An early, and short-lived, attempt at a religious headdress. The Teresians appeared in them one morning, but Father Walsh called Sister Mary Joseph aside and said succinctly, "Take off those headache bands."

15

The family grows. On July 4, 1918, there were twenty-six Sisters and a dog. The Community kept growing, though they were still waiting for permission from Rome to begin their formal religious training.

"No sooner had I decided to enter Maryknoll than my spiritual strength seemed to vanish. I hoped I'd never make it. I hoped I'd be run over before I got home. Once at home, I hoped I'd fall and break my neck! My director, too, discouraged me from joining a group that was not officially recognized. But with the help of our Blessed Mother I overcame all obstacles and in May, 1916, I left home with one suitcase of belongings and enough money to get me to Maryknoll. My feelings on tearing myself away from my dearly loved family were exactly those of Thérèse of Lisieux: 'I did not shed a tear,' she wrote, 'but the beating of my heart became so violent that I wondered if I were going to die. Oh, the agony of that moment! One must have gone through it to understand.' How many a heart has shared the little Saint's experience!"

Newcomers were still given the habit and a religious name. On February 25, 1918, the latest three became Sisters Paul, Michael, and Thomas, bringing the number of Sisters to twenty-one. At the little ceremony a Maryknoll Father said that, though the habit was not pretty, it was much more important that it was God's livery. Outside the chapel an indignant Sister Francis gasped, "Imagine his saying that our habit isn't pretty!" Many years later, Mother Mary Joseph experienced the same indignation when a priest in Hawaii contrasted the life of the Sisters with that of an actress who had tragically committed suicide. "She had money, attention, beauty," said Father, "but she was so unhappy she killed herself. Now you see before you" — they were in the first row—"the Maryknoll Sisters. They are poor, they are not noticed, they are not beautiful, but they are happy." When this was repeated to Mother, she said, "My Sisters *are* beautiful."

The 1918 flu epidemic hit Maryknoll, and it was a very serious thing for the little Community. When nearly half of the group became ill, Father Superior decided that to keep it from spreading, the Sisters who were ill should stay at St. Teresa's, but the others should move to the dormitory above the *Field Afar* offices. There was only one nurse, Sister Elizabeth; and two of the newest postulants, Sister John and Sister James (Sister Mary Joseph's own sister), were assigned to assist her, one during the night, the other during the day. The office work and the cooking still had to be coped with, but the rector of the Seminary sent word that the seminarians would do the laundry themselves, not only their own but also anything the Sisters needed done as well. This resulted in a few laughs to cheer the Sisters up. First an apologetic seminarian arrived at the front door with something that looked like a small tent. It was a Sister's habit, starched and scorched to a dapple brown. "I washed it twice over, but it still comes out this color," said the perplexed student. Later a Sister returned from work to find a neat little gray package waiting for her—her clean habit folded in careful creases to the size of a handkerchief! The sheets too were carefully ironed and folded into small squares.

When the epidemic had barely passed, Sister Mary Joseph received a call for help from the Graymoor Sisters nearby. Of their thirty Sisters, only four were well. "My Sisters are all up and about," Sister reassured them, and sent her only nurse, Sister Elizabeth, and another Sister to help her.

The following spring when she herself had to go to Baltimore for a long-delayed operation, Sister Mary Joseph insisted that Sister Elizabeth, the nurse, remain with the Community. Sister Mary Joseph left with a big smile and some last-minute instructions on canning and cooking. However, the operation was serious, and she was gone for eleven long weeks. Her homecoming was a gala event. Despite the "work-as-usual" schedule, the Sisters found time to fashion an archway of real flowers to express their joy at her return. Once she was back, she admitted she often would have given a great deal to see a Maryknoll habit standing in the doorway of her hospital room.

In June, 1919, they sent the third petition to

Rome. Sister Fidelia, a Sinsinawa Dominican, came that month to begin the Sisters' training in the Dominican way of life, while they waited again to see if the Holy See would give permission to open a novitiate. Thirteen of the Sisters had been permitted to take private vows such as lay people may take in the world, but the group had as yet no standing as a Congregation. Sister Mary Joseph explained that Sister Fidelia was the superior and that all must go to her for permissions. However, when she arrived, Sister Fidelia was quick to assure the Sisters that she would take charge of spiritual matters only and that everything else would be in Sister Mary Joseph's jurisdiction. Sister Fidelia loved Sister Mary Joseph. The cooperation of these two women made the good work possible and provided a splendid example of obedience to the Community. Each morning, when work assignments were given out, Sister Mary Joseph never failed to turn first to Sister Fidelia and ask, "May I give some directions to the Sisters?"

In October of that year, the Sisters were all hoping to celebrate Sister Mary Joseph's birthday, but thought that perhaps as real-honest-to-goodness Religious they would have to forego it. All wanted to ask Sister Fidelia's permission, but not one of them could find the courage. They let it go until the very day, when Sister John, one of the newest members, went to Sister and blurted out: "Today is Sister Mary Joseph's birthday. May we celebrate?"

"Today is Sister's birthday," came the quick remonstrance, "and nobody told me? Of course you may celebrate it, and you must celebrate it every year. Sister is the foundress of this Community."

And they did. In no time the Community room at St. Teresa's was decorated, with crepe paper strung from one corner to another. In obedience to Father Superior's happy direction, "Make a difference between a feast and a fast-day meal," they hurried down to Ossining and bought ice cream. In half an hour they had a tremendous party going. When Sister Fidelia

joined the festivities she could hardly believe her eyes. "I never saw a Community," she said with a smile, "that could get a party going so quickly." This particular ability is a Maryknoll virtue to this day.

Parties were made up of simple family fun. Someone played the piano, someone recited, someone presented a dramatic monologue, and everyone sang.

Much of the support for the Sisters came from women interested in mission work, who wished to help in some way. They organized into Mission Circles around the country. They ran card parties, from the proceeds of which they supplied sacristy linens, as well as table and bed linens. In the summer of 1919, it was decided to have a little get-together for the chairwomen of these groups, both as a way of saying thank you to them for their generous work, and to give them a chance to exchange ideas on the best means of spreading interest in the missions. A weekend was planned for them, and the Sisters all moved out of their quarters in the *Field Afar* building and crowded back into St. Teresa's to make room for the visitors.

The weekend was a huge success. Groups continued to come throughout the rest of the summer, sometimes for the weekend, sometimes only for the day. One group arrived from a distance on Sunday to spend just the afternoon. They were unexpected, and no provision for lunch had been made for them. Sister Mary Joseph told the Sisters to set up tables and chairs outdoors, and there she served her guests the Community supper. Not only did the visitors receive the usual Maryknoll hospitality; the Community enjoyed raiding the icebox to make a supper of leftovers.

The visit to Maryknoll had an unforeseen result—vocations to the Sisterhood. For example, Rose Hartman was invited by Sister Catherine, who had charge of the groups then, to come to Maryknoll to meet leaders of other Mission Circles on August 15, 1919. Among the fourteen women who came were Elizabeth Tarpey from

Philadelphia, who became Mother Mary Columba, second Mother General; Sara Jane Kelly of Tarrytown, New York, who became Sister Christine; and Gertrude Miltenberger of Pittsburgh, who was later Sister M. Clare.

Before she left Pittsburgh, Rose had gone to her spiritual director, a Passionist priest, and told him she felt she wanted to apply to enter Maryknoll. Because the group was not yet recognized by the Holy See, Father hesitated to encourage her. However, he said, "See Father Walsh and speak to him about it." Rose did; she also spoke to Sister Mary Joseph with whom she had been in correspondence about it. Thus it was that Sister Mary Joseph invited her to stay a few days after the others left.

On the 22nd of August, around noon, Rose was planning to leave Maryknoll. Sister Mary Joseph was at a meeting of the Community's Council. Rose stood on the porch at St. Teresa's with Sister Ambrose. "Oh, dear, I shall have to leave without saying goodbye to Sister Mary Joseph," she grieved. Because the taxi was at the door to take her to the train, she could stay no longer.

At that moment Sister Mary Joseph came out of the house, opened her arms, and took Rose into them. "You've been accepted," she said. "When do you want to come?"

Rose ran out to the taxi with flying feet and took the train back to Pittsburgh. She entered the following December 7th, and became Sister

On mailing day, crowded quarters sent the Sisters outside to get The Field Afar *ready for distribution. By 1920 they wore the now well-known Maryknoll veil. Postulants wore the gray cotton habit with mesh veils.*

Mary Veronica. Elizabeth Tarpey entered the same day.

Throughout this period Sister Mary Joseph showed a characteristic breadth of vision. She wished her Sisters to be as well educated as means would allow. In spite of all the work, six Sisters were sent to Ossining Hospital to take a course in practical nursing. Many times they walked the long hill back to Maryknoll, and in the winter they sometimes went down by sleigh. When the opportunity presented itself, another group went to study chant at Pius X School.

For those with no previous experience in Church music, this was hard work indeed, and they often asked Mother to be excused. Her answer was, "You take it and study it even if you fail." The ability and opportunity to sing chant have proved one of the Community's greatest joys and a tremendous mission talent for introducing new Christians to the liturgy of the Church. Even as early as 1913, in obedience to St. Pius X's wishes for the Church, the Mass was sung in Community, with the Seminarians and the Sisters alternating.

Our first missioners departed in 1920 to work with the Japanese on the West Coast. Sister Teresa and Sister Gemma went to Seattle, and Sister Magdalen and Sister Aloysius headed for Los Angeles. They now had their complete habit, including a white Dominican scapular beneath the gray one, and a Chi-Rho, symbol of Maryknoll, embroidered in blue at the end of the cincture.

Sister Mary Joseph's own sister, Sister James, showed musical talent and was assigned to study music. She worked a large part of the day at the *Field Afar* offices and then hurried to the convent to practice on the piano. Every week she and Sister Raphael, a singer, caught the train to New York City for lessons.

Another class instituted at Sister Mary Joseph's suggestion was one in Church History given by Father Phelan, pastor at Brewster, New York, who taught the Maryknoll seminarians. He came once a week to teach when the Sisters had completed their desk work, manual work, and prayers. Father had a restful voice, and more than one Sister fell asleep during these periods. Sister John, whose work included keeping lists of Maryknoll sponsors, was among these culprits. "I remember one day Father was talking about Venerable Bede as I fell asleep. I dreamt there and then that Father Superior put his head in the classroom window and asked me if the Venerable Bede was on our sponsor list. I looked up and told him, 'No.' He replied in the dream, 'Put him on by all means, and make him a Perpetual Member.' "

When 1920 arrived, although they had begun to be filled with the spirit of St. Dominic, they still could not officially call themselves his children. However, that was only because God was waiting for the right day. On February 14, 1920, the long-awaited and much-prayed-for document arrived approving them as a religious institute. On that day they began the formal canonical novitiate, which would give them the privilege a year later to take public vows. On that day there were thirty-nine women at Maryknoll. Six had already given eight years to the Congregation. All had come to help, most of them with only discouragement from families and pastors alike; they came with no assurance that they would ever be able to fulfill their treasured missionary vocations.

But their dreams were coming true. They had everything to look forward to.

*Four faces heavenward! Children of the Loting
Mission in China, the Maryknoll Sisters' first
territory in the Orient. The orphans were given
a schooling far superior to that of most girls in
China.*

II

God Gave Increase / 1920 to 1938

As soon as the approval from Rome arrived on February 14, 1920, the canonical year of novitiate began. A quarter-century later, Mother Mary Joseph told her novices the ideal of a Maryknoll Sister she had formed in her own heart. "I would have her distinguished," Mother said, "by Christlike charity, a limpid simplicity of soul, heroic generosity, selflessness, unswerving loyalty, prudent zeal, an orderly mind, gracious courtesy, an adaptable disposition, solid piety, and the saving grace of a sense of humor."

"We are seeking souls," Mother urged at another time. "For this we need all our individuality, all our generosity, all our graciousness and sweetness and simplicity, all our powers of gentle persuasiveness, in fact, all of the things which the good God has given to us. Each one of us in her own work, with her own particular attractiveness, . . . must cultivate her natural gifts on a spiritual plane."

Holiness was the whole of it. And holiness at Maryknoll had the meaning of wholeness sanctified anew by the Spirit of Christ.

The new congregation did not flag a moment in generosity. In April, 1920, Bishop Cantwell of Los Angeles, and shortly thereafter Bishop

O'Dea of Seattle, asked for help for their Japanese parishioners, and four Sisters went out at once to these first mission posts.

On July 2, 1920, the Congregation was formally affiliated with the Dominican Order. The Master General called them St. Dominic's crown, because they fulfilled the Saint's ardent wish to have in his religious family a branch entirely dedicated to foreign missions.

The tiny chapel in St. Teresa's was the scene of the first profession ceremony on February 15, 1921. Twenty-three Sisters made the simple vows of poverty, chastity, and obedience. Sister Mary Joseph was appointed Mother Superior, and was thereafter called Mother, while Sister Fidelia of Sinsinawa continued to be novice mistress until August, 1924, when she returned to her own Community. In August, 1921, the remaining Sisters of the first group made their vows, bringing the number of professed to thirty-nine Sisters.

Vocations began to pour in. Fifty-nine women entered the postulancy in 1920. Sister Fidelia said frankly: "God is giving you outstanding vocations of great talent. My own Community would be happy to accept them."

was interspersed with considerable strictly American giggling. The teacher was very dis-edified, and Sister Paul decided we had to get our own regular teacher. Eveutually we got one from Canton, Anna Tsang, and she brought a lot of enthusiasm to her teaching."

The Sisters began to think about works they could engage in to provide support for their convent. With one frame on which to produce hand-embroidered vestments, they started an industrial shop in one of the downstairs rooms. Their chief helper in getting this going was Teresa Yeung, who in 1927 entered Maryknoll and became Sister Maria Teresa. As time went on, the industrial room became more and more important, providing work for many women and creating vestments that became sought after in many parts of the world. The Sisters were also delighted that many of the young women who were trained in this department later entered religious Communities, including Carmel and the Precious Blood Sisters.

At Christmastime, the Sisters found themselves remembered in many heartwarming ways. Father J. E. Walsh sent a portable organ and Mass vestments. The people, both Portuguese and Chinese, sent gifts, especially of food. Their first midnight Mass was celebrated in their tiny convent chapel that was just large enough for the altar, the priest, and the Sisters' six prie-dieux.

Sister Paul's great emphasis in these early mission days was on personal holiness, and she spared nothing to provide the Sisters with real formative assistance. Even in their poverty, she found the means to get a Jesuit Father to come from the Philippines in 1922 to give the Sisters' retreat. Father John Hanley, an American Paulist priest, sent a fully equipped library from a house that had been closed. One of the most-read books in the house had been recommended by Father James E. Walsh—it was *Village Life in China*.

October, 1922, brought six more Sisters from Maryknoll where sixteen had recently made their vows, bringing the number of professed Sisters in the Community to fifty-five. Led by Sister Magdalen, the new group included Sisters Francis, Dolores, Cecilia, Thomas, and Gertrude, who was a registered nurse. For a little while the Hong Kong house was bursting. However, some were destined for a brand-new mission — Yeungkong — where Father Francis X. Ford was pastor. Sister Paul accompanied them on this first trip, and they found work aplenty waiting for them — a school for blind and crippled children, a crèche for abandoned babies, a small dispensary, an old-folks' home, and the ever-urgent language study.

"If I remember correctly," Sister Rose writes, "we left Hong Kong on November 19th and arrived at the Yeungkong mission on the 22nd. Sister Magdalen was in charge of the group. While we were still in Hong Kong, Sister Paul had sent Sister Imelda and me to the French Hospital for some practical training in nursing. Sister Lawrence had received the same type of training at the Ossining Hospital at home.

"Sister Gertrude was put in charge of the dispensary with Sister Lawrence to help her. At the outskirts of the mission property were fourteen old ladies living in huts who went out every day to beg for their upkeep. Sister Gertrude got busy and had all the old ladies take a bath. Then she moved them into empty rooms of a house in which Father Ford had already established the crèche and the school for blind or crippled children. Within a month of our arrival, all our charges were located in this one building.

"There were thirty boxes in the crèche that served as cribs for the infants, and there were already 20 babies in them, each tabbed with the name Rose. Naturally this aroused our curiosity. Then we found out it was Father Ford's mother's name.

"I remember telling Sister Paul the previous

Thanks be to God, pray the little blind children, abandoned by their parents because of this defect, who found a home and tender loving care at Loting under Sister Candida Maria.

Babies abandoned on doorsteps and in trash barrels were often so far gone there was little hope of survival. Here some of the older orphans at Loting, China, hold the tiny mites while the priest baptizes them.

June: 'Here I have been studying for almost nine months, and I don't feel I know a thing about this language. How can I learn it?' 'I don't know, Sister,' she answered. 'Do the best you can!' Now, since I was supposed to know a little Chinese, I was given charge of the old folks and the orphans, with Sister Francis and our catechist and language teacher, Anna Tsang, to help me. We kept up the study too.

"I felt we were there for souls, so I tried to interest the women in God and religion as they came to visit us. We found that the people came to look at the house, but that was the end of it. Then I discovered that if we visited them in their homes, they would make a return call. I asked Father Ford if I could do this with a woman catechist and he gladly acquiesced. My first companion, Mrs. Mok, had bound feet. That meant a fifteen-minute trip took us an hour and a quarter, so I decided I needed a more

agile companion. During the year, one of our school girls, about eighteen years old, became a Catholic, so I trained her as a catechist and she became my companion. We spent quite a bit of time thinking up excuses to make these home visits. We went to see friends of our Catholics. We visited the women who were wet-nurses for our orphaned babies. Besides making more friends, we learned many things about village homelife.

"Sister Gertrude," Sister Rose recounts, "had been attending the dispensary besides studying the language, and getting used to the customs and climate. It was a colossal job and must have been just too much. She caught typhoid from one of the boys at the school. Toward the end of July Sister became ill. She was to renew her vows on August 4th, but by then she was so ill she could not go to the chapel. It was August 18th before we knew she had typhoid, although I think she herself suspected it. We were to go to Hong Kong for the yearly retreat, but Sister Paul decided three of us should remain to care for Sister. On August 21st, however, I joined the passengers on the river junk for Hong Kong. During the night I awoke

with a start. I knew immediately that Sister Gertrude had died. The catechist caught up with the junk in the morning and told us of her death. I immediately returned to Yeungkong where Sister was buried on August 22nd. Then all of us left again for Hong Kong, bringing the news of our first Maryknoll Sister's death on the missions."

The Hong Kong convent had moved to a more spacious house, with a garage that was turned into the industrial department. The Sisters taught music to several children, including one Alfred Williams, who years later became a Trappist monk in South Wales. In the fall, Mother Mary Joseph arrived on visitation, bringing with her seven more Sisters. When she returned to the States she took Aurea Xavier with her to become the first Maryknoll postulant from China. Aurea is now Sister Chanel. First, however, Mother spent Christmas with her Hong Kong family.

At work or play the orphans at Loting enjoyed themselves and one another. The water-carrying brigade (bottom, opposite page) *and the grass-cutting detail* (above) *were steady part-time jobs. The littlest ones* (top, opposite page) *amble through Loting's famous moon gate with Sister Francis.*

Hm-mm, good! A youngster in Loting handles chopsticks with a deftness that amazes the un-initiated missioners.

Before her return, she and Sister Paul went up through China and Manchuria to Korea, where Maryknoll's Father Patrick Byrne was asking for Maryknoll Sisters.

Father Byrne met the travelers in Mukden, Manchuria, and brought them down into Korea. There, on February 11, 1924, on the feast of Our Lady of Lourdes, in a tiny mud-walled house converted into a temporary chapel, Mother and Sister Paul made their religious vows for life.

Before leaving Korea, Mother promised Father Byrne she would send Sisters for the work there. Sisters Lucy, Eugenia, Juliana, Sylvester, Andrew, and Augustine arrived on October 21, 1924. Their new home was Gishu in the north of Korea on the Yalu River, a city of mud huts with straw roofs—or tile, if the owner was affluent. Right in the middle of town was the Catholic church—a red-brick Gothic building. The convent, too, was red brick, high-ceilinged and hard to heat.

There was so much to get used to, it was hard to know where to begin. The icy cold winter of Korea had arrived. The local food consisted of rice, millet, and cabbage. Meat could be obtained only on market day, which was every fifth day. There was the now traditional difficulty of obtaining water, the difficulty that had begun for the Sisters at the snake-filled Hawthorne well. Here in Korea they had running water—cold, of course—obtained from a tank on the upper floor to which it had been hand pumped. Because the Korean cold froze bread dough before it was baked and it would not rise, bread had to be "imported" for the Sisters once a week from Shingishu, a town thirty miles away. But hard as these things were, they found the good also—the things that sparked their keen sense of humor, that gave them joy in little events, that evoked their interest in everything new and strange in their surroundings. They delighted in the white-dressed men and women, in the men with high-crowned black horsehair hats and long thin pipes, in the long thick braids of the girls, their delicately colored silk "best" dresses, their wonderful holiday swinging contests.

The hard things were as obvious as they were unexpected: to be patient, humble, cheerful, and charitable in the face of the tedious routine of language study and the frustrating attempts to communicate with their new neighbors.

Their language teacher was Mrs. Helen Chang, wife of artist Louis Chang. His brother, John Chang, became South Korea's first Ambassador to Washington, Vice President under Syngman Rhee, and later Premier of the country. His sister, Mary, was already in the Maryknoll novitiate, and would become Sister Mary Agneta. With her was Magdalena Kim, another Korean girl, who became Sister Margaret.

One of the Maryknoll Sisters was assigned to learn Japanese, since there was a fair-sized Japanese population in Korea. Her teacher was a former Buddhist girl, Nakamura San, who was converted to the Faith, and four years later entered Maryknoll to become Sister Sabina. These vocations later proved immensely valuable to the Sisters' mission work in the Orient during World War II.

As always, the Sisters found their work ready and waiting for them: a dispensary was set up, an old-folks' home had already been established, and catechetical work was begun.

EXPANSION IN CHINA

As the work in Korea began, that in China expanded. Sisters Paul and Imelda accompanied a new group of pioneers on a five-day trip upriver on a sampan, an outsized rowboat with woven straw covering. Their destination was Loting, Maryknoll Father Daniel McShane's territory. At the mission the Sisters found an orphanage and a crèche. When they were happily established, Sisters Paul and Imelda returned overland through bandit territory, and arrived in Hong Kong in time to welcome six new Mary-

knoll Sisters. The Community in China in 1924 numbered twenty-five.

At the urging of Hong Kong's Portuguese Catholics, the Sisters opened a kindergarten. The only place available was the Sisters' community room, and here twelve little girls began their preschool work under the guidance of Sister Liguori. This was the beginning of Maryknoll Convent School.

Older students of Holy Spirit School, shown here with Sister Santa Maria. Subjects here were taught in Chinese and English. At Maryknoll Convent School, also in Hong Kong, subjects were taught in English.

Kindergartners—all of Chinese parentage—at Holy Spirit School in 1934. The school was an old building on "The Rock," the center island of Hong Kong Harbor.

Three who set the course aright (left to right): Sister Mary Fidelia of the Sinsinawa Dominicans trained Maryknoll Sisters for the religious life; Mother Mary Joseph founded the Congregation and was Mother General for twenty-five years; Sister Mary Magdalen, a missioner in China until 1925, returned to become novice mistress and subsequently first superior of the Maryknoll Sisters' Cloister, started in 1932.

Six of the many stalwart souls whose hard work and prayers helped found Maryknoll. Left to right, they are Sister Anna Maria who entered in 1912 from Boston; Sister Mary Anthony from Danbury, Connecticut, in 1915; Sister Theophane, Father Walsh's secretary before entering from Boston in 1912; Sister Philomena, from New York in 1918; Sister Thomas from Holyoke, Massachusetts, in 1917; and Mother Mary Joseph, who led them all.

Back in the States the Community had its first General Chapter in 1925. Mother Mary Joseph was elected the Community's Mother General, with Sister Columba as First Councilor; Sister St. John, Second; Sister Mary de Paul, Third; Sister Felicita, Fourth, and Secretary-General. Sister Magdalen was recalled to Maryknoll from Yeungkong to be the novice mistress.

Agneta Chang, sister of John Chang, former president of South Korea, as a postulant in 1922 with Sister Gemma. As Sister Mary Agneta she died under the Communists in 1950 in Korea. A plaque in the Motherhouse chapel commemorates her heroism.

Even in the 1920's Maryknoll attracted vocations from the Orient. The photo (above) shows
Phyllis Wong, later Sister Teresita; her aunt,
Sister Maria Teresa, then a novice; and their
friend Lolly Carvalho, who became Sister Cecilia Marie. These three girls were from Hong
Kong. (Below) Three Korean friends, daughters
of old Catholic families, who entered together
(left to right): Sister Margaret, Sister Clara, and
Sister Agneta.

On April 30, 1926, a windblown procession of
novices and postulants march to the seminary
where, in the chapel, they will advance one step
further in the religious life.

34

A funeral in the old days. The body of Sister Emmanuel (Donahue) is carried on the shoulders of Maryknoll Brothers from the little stone chapel, St. Martha's. The immediate family follows. Sister died on May 9, 1923.

The first mission group assigned to China in 1921. Seated, left to right, are Sister Lawrence, Sister Paul, superior, and Sister Rose. Standing, left to right, are Sister Imelda, Sister Barbara, and Sister Monica.

Switchboard operator Sister Patricia (right) used slack moments to work on embroidery that would be sold or would serve as a bridge-party prize to help the mission cause. This picture was taken in 1922 or early 1923.

The old pharmacy where Sister Georgea saved the Community a pretty penny compounding medicines. Sister worked here from 1922 to 1927 when she was assigned to the Philippines.

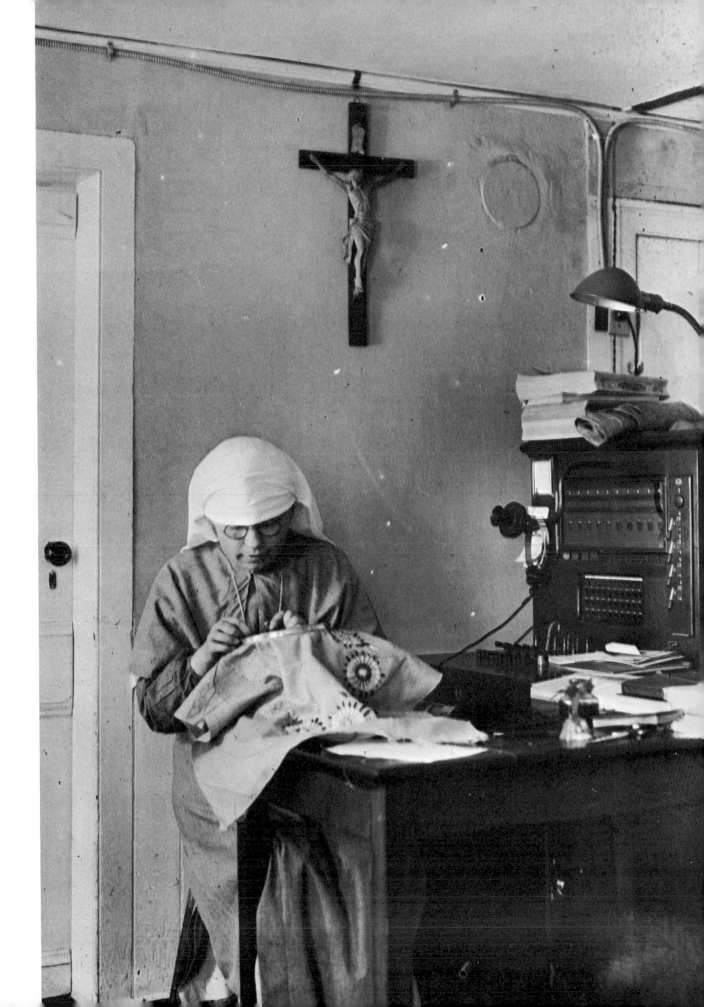

Before the days of walk-in freezers, the kitchen detail included long hours of preparing, cooking, and canning everything that could be grown to last the Community through the winter.

*Methods course in simple cooking! Just a side-
line for Sister Charles and Mother Mary Joseph,
but very important to the young priests headed
for China and Korea, where they would run the
hazard of ruined health through improper use
of food.*

During spring, summer, and fall, in 1928, evening
recreation was enjoyed under the tall trees, with
laughter shared over the day's funny events.
Two shy Sisters erected an umbrella to shield
themselves from the nosy camera.

Father James A. Walsh, co-founder of the
Maryknoll Fathers, always had time to stop and
talk with the Sisters. Here he is with Sister
Teresita, a native of Hong Kong, in 1930.

About 1926, space indoors was at a premium, so Sister Leo (right) set up her cassock-cleaning department outdoors. With inflammable cleaner it was a safety move too.

Father Cotta, the Sisters' chaplain, was an able and amusing photographer, and Mother was his favorite model. His trick photo (left) shows her in six spots around St. Joseph's Convent.

It was always good fun to be with Mother, and she delighted in her novices, shown with her here outside St. Martha's Chapel in 1927.

BACK IN CHINA

Meanwhile, in China the Sisters experienced the first political upheavals that were to follow them throughout the years. The antiforeign strike that had begun in Shanghai spread to the interior, and the Sisters were forced to evacuate Yeungkong and Loting. After lengthy negotiations an American gunboat was dispatched to Yeungkong, and brought the Sisters safely to Hong Kong. Sometime later the Loting Sisters were also evacuated.

PHILIPPINES

Early in 1926 Sister Paul accompanied Sisters Lumena and Dolorita to the Philippines to look into the possibility of accepting Archbishop Michael J. O'Doherty's request for American Sisters to begin a Teacher-Training School.

Maryknoll Sisters reached Manila on January 22, 1926. They stayed with Mother Helen and the Assumption Sisters, who were to be their generous friends. Next morning they went out to the school, a former Augustinian monastery in Malabon in the province of Rizal about ten miles from Manila. They met the pastor of the parish of San Bartolomeo, Father José Paguia, whose humble delight at having them come warmed their hearts.

After Sister Paul had returned to Hong Kong, Sisters Lumena and Dolorita set to work directing repairs on the old monastery and visiting the neighborhood. There were two Protestant churches and several Aglipayan, a schismatic sect that had undermined Philippine Catholicism for a quarter-century. Many of the townspeople worked either in a cigar or a candy factory. A nearby town had a small shipyard that boasted the only telephone in the area. There was also a sugar refinery. But most of the people were farmers or fishermen.

The Filipino people, with typical graciousness, visited often, bringing gifts of fruit and offering their services. The Sisters saw their first Filipino lunch break. The men built a picnic fire

Reading a story to Chinese children on the roadside was part of the Direct Apostolate practiced in Bishop Ford's Kaying area. Sister Madeleine Sophie has gathered a typical crowd to hear the story of the Christ Child.

45

over which they steamed a pot of rice seasoned with small fish. After the meal, each took time out for a short siesta under a shade tree.

On April 1, 1926, Sisters Raphael and Marie de Lourdes arrived on loan from Hong Kong. They brought with them a set of reed furniture for the convent living room. The work of rebuilding was just finished, and the Sisters decided to move on Easter Saturday, April 4th. In the midst of making these arrangements they received the happy news that Father Superior James A. Walsh would arrive on Easter Sunday. Lest they be allowed to catch their breath, on Friday afternoon Archbishop O'Doherty came for an informal tour and to bless the building. Nevertheless they managed the move the next day.

Easter morning brought Father Superior for a short visit, since he had to spend most of the day in Manila. However, he left his Mass kit and returned early on Easter Monday to offer the first Mass in the new convent. The reed table served as an altar in the unfurnished chapel. The Sisters were overjoyed to have Father there. He spoke seriously to them on the text "Unless the grain of wheat falling into the ground die, itself remaineth alone." He believed that with headwinds in the beginning, their mission would be firmly founded in Faith.

Things began to move in May, when registrations were held for the primary, intermediate, and Normal School departments. Sister Augustine arrived unexpectedly from Korea, and was enjoying her breakfast next morning when the cable announcing her imminent approach was delivered. On June 3, 1926, the faculty arrived in the persons of Sisters Teresita, Philip, de Sales, de Chantal, and Assumpta, with three more to come after earning their Master's degrees in the States. They began teaching on the 7th, thereby initiating the second Maryknoll mission tradition. (The water problem had, of course, presented itself as usual. There were two sources, a rain barrel and a well in the backyard, both of which were more often empty than

full.) The new movement became known as the "latecomers' early start." New arrivals to mission lands inevitably came just in time to start teaching. (The record to date is held by two Sister-teachers who left the Motherhouse in New York Friday afternoon and jet-planed to Hong Kong, where they began teaching Monday morning.)

Three hundred students appeared at the Malabon school that Monday morning in June, 1926. There was not a single desk for them, and there were rented chairs sufficient only for the grade-school department. At the end of July, Sisters Angela, Theodore, and Caritas arrived and began teaching the following day. The subsequent rearrangement of teachers brought about the Sisters' first experience with the wholehearted, affectionate Filipino spirit. After only two months, Sister Philip's class were heartbroken over the loss of their little Madre when she was transferred to another grade. Later, when Sister Augustine went to Hong Kong, her pupils showed the same deep sense of loss, and several of them cut class to go to the pier to say goodbye. Again, when summer came, far from wanting to leave school, the children sobbed and insisted they could not live through the summer without the Sisters.

Then began the troubles for which Father Superior had prepared them. Sister Teresita became seriously ill, and was found to have tuberculosis. Three of the other Sisters suddenly collapsed with the dengue—"breakbone" fever. In the midst of this, as they were juggling Sisters to cover classes and nurse the sick, Mr. William Buckisch, the American Director of Private Schools, arrived, bringing with him Mr. Lino Castillejo, who would later take over his job. Sister Augustine gave these visitors a demonstration of first-grade teaching that so impressed them that they asked if there were not some way to keep Sister in the Philippines. Mr. Buckisch recommended sports, particularly tennis and volleyball, to restore the Sisters' health. Throughout his administration he showed the most generous and cooperative interest in the Sisters' work.

Sister Mercedes arrived from Hong Kong to nurse Sister Teresita. She brought news of a new work begun in Kongmoon under Sister Imelda's direction—a novitiate for a local Community. Eventually Sister Teresita went to the Baguio mountains, where the better climate was expected to help her recover.

Growing acquaintance with the people revealed their beautiful devotion to the Blessed Mother, and the many loving practices by which they expressed their affection for God and His beloved saints. However, they were not at all vitally conscious of the Blessed Sacrament in their midst. They enjoyed processions, and work in the town would be suspended while one took place. Holy Week had a whole series of services. In the church, a figure of the Christ was raised upon a cross by sweating, shirtless men in an almost frightening representation of the crucifixion. However, when the figure was in place, one sweat-drenched laborer bent over simply and kissed the pierced feet. The procession of the Risen Christ on Holy Saturday afternoon took three hours. The climax came when the two groups carrying the statue of Our Lord and that of Our Lady met. The black cloak that covered the Madonna's brilliant blue gown was then removed, and the groups united joyfully to carry the two statues side by side back to the church.

The Sisters' first annual retreat was somewhat less than calm. Classes went on as usual, but since Thanksgiving Day occurred that week, the Sisters were looking forward to having—so they thought—at least a long weekend of quiet. Early Thanksgiving morning a group was baptized, and afterward two Sisters not making the retreat had a small party in a classroom for the nine new Christians and their families. Shortly after they left the school, stones from the old church tower crashed down into the building destroying two classrooms, including the one they had just left. At first the Sisters thought two of their guests were still in the building. When they were sure no one was injured, they sent word to the Archbishop. "Thank God no one is injured," was his immediate comment. "If anything had happened to the Maryknoll Sisters, I would resign." This undoubtedly referred to the criticism he had suffered in bringing them to his diocese. The Archbishop came out as soon as he could to view the damage, which appalled him, and to make arrangements for repairs. In the midst of all this excitement, a Mr. Copyn, the Dutch manager of the local sugar refinery, arrived with his daughter to ask if the Sisters could start that day giving her English lessons. It was just the touch of humor they needed to help them recover.

Then good news came. Mother Mary Joseph was on her way to visit them. When gentle Father Paguia told this to the people, he gave a little talk in Tagalog calling the Sisters "the angels from America." He had altar boys spotted along the road to send back word of Mother's arrival, and as soon as she neared the town the church bells pealed out a welcome. After giving Benediction in the parish church, Father Paguia hurried to the front steps, where to Mother's chagrin and amazement he expressed the depth of his gratitude by taking her hand and kissing it. The Sisters were thrilled to have Mother with them, and she in turn showed her ever-thoughtful concern by making arrangements for them to spend the Christmas holiday in the refreshing Baguio mountains. Just at this time a convent of discalced Carmelites was opened in Manila, and the two Communities agreed to set aside the feasts of Our Lady of Mount Carmel and St. Dominic to pray for each other.

The new year, 1927, brought an expansion to their mission responsibilities in the Philippines. They were asked to take over St. Paul's Hospital and St. Mary's Residence Hall, both in Manila. The former included a school to train nurses; the latter was a hostel for Catholic students attending the Philippine Normal School and the

University of the Philippines. Sister Columba was assigned to be mission superior of the now varied works in the Philippines.

HONG KONG

Continuing her travels, Mother Mary Joseph went on to the Hong Kong convents where she found excitement aplenty. In November, 1926, the Yeungkong Sisters had begun their return journey to that mission. They went aboard a new steamer on its first run, and at Ngaimoon, pirates, disguised as first-class passengers, came aboard. When the ship was about five hours out of Kongmoon, the pirates took over, killing six of the crew. They sailed the steamer onto a sandbar, and for two days steadily ransacked her. The Sisters waited in the cabin, and after a while the pirates came, holding guns in their faces and demanding their money and goods. They had a large mission shipment with them, since they had decided to bring back a year's supply of basic necessities. The pirates took it all, and returned periodically with new demands for money and goods. The experience was so harrowing that the Sisters' catechist, Alphonsine Chan, who was with them, had a mental breakdown as a result. On their final visit, unable to discover anything else, the pirates demanded Sister Francis' new shoes. But she had had enough. Guns or no guns, she steadfastly refused to part with them. But they won out and took the shoes off her feet. She was never to hear the end of it. All around the world she could be sure that her Maryknoll Sisters would greet her with a big smile, and ask, "Have you got your shoes safe, Sister Francis?"

However, new works were at hand. In Hong Kong the Sisters opened Holy Spirit School for 120 Chinese girls, with the subjects taught in Chinese and English. Maryknoll Convent School, which was growing apace, accepted students of all nationalities. The subjects were taught in English.

PHILIPPINES

Some of the Hong Kong Sisters were transferred to the Philippines to help with the new works. Several pilot projects were begun at the Normal School at Malabon. In-training service for teachers was inaugurated by Sisters Theodore and Caritas, who went to Lucena to give a course in Catholic Action to that town's public-school teachers. The Sisters included the Red Cross Home Nursing course as part of the Normal School curriculum, and two Filipino nurses came to give the instructions. Sister Philip began a manual-training department for the boys, including instruction in bookbinding.

In all the missions emphasis was placed on a Catholic atmosphere. The Sisters began to take some of the senior students with them to do catechetical work in the barrios, and this grew into a major Catholic Action program. They decided then to have a retreat day for the students, which was a fine success in spite of the fact that the retreat master wasn't able to come and one of the Sisters had to give the conferences herself. They began a special course in the sacramental character of marriage, since the holiness of this vocation seemed generally misunderstood.

The Sisters on their part strove to appreciate the culture of the people they worked with, and they discovered and adopted several beautiful religious customs of the Philippines. They accompanied the children to the cemeteries on All Souls' Day, and eventually the children on their part began that day with Mass, to the great delight of the new pastor, Father Mercado, appointed after Padre Paguia's sudden death.

The custom of "visiting" on fiestas suited the Sisters perfectly. Now that they had three missions in the area, it was a treat to have periodic reunions at the Malabon house.

At Christmastime they learned of the beautiful Filipino art of forming bamboo into star shapes and decorating the spokes with brilliantly colored paper and festoons to commemorate the

Sister Marie Marquette (above) *shows off triplets born at St. Paul's Hospital in Manila. The hospital was one of the Maryknoll Sisters' first works in the Philippines.*

St. Jude's Patronage, a charitable "arm" of St. Paul's Hospital, Manila, provided food and medical care to hundreds, and, in cases where the breadwinner of a family was laid up for a long time, paid the rent and bought clothes for the wife and children. The photo (below), *taken in the late 1930's, shows Sister Georgea and Sister Frederica.*

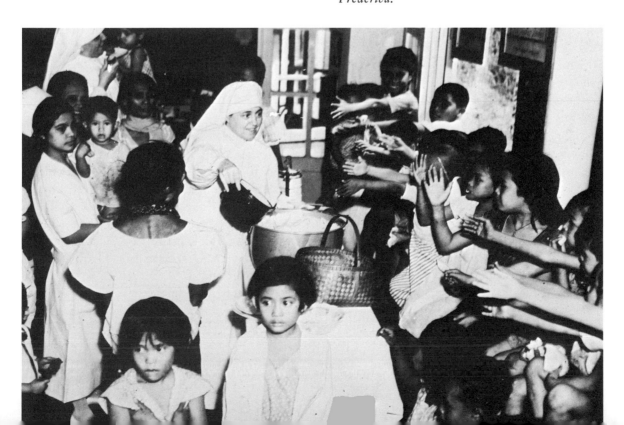

star that led the Gentiles to the King of Israel. Much to the children's great joy, the Sisters asked them to make stars for the convent and even for their chapel.

They took the children on as many class trips as possible. One group went to the forestry and agricultural school at Los Banos, little suspecting that this would be the Sisters' grim "home" where they were to be interned during World War II. They also brought the older students to St. Paul's Hospital for open-house day, during which doctors and nurses explained their professions.

When Sister Eucharista began to include religion methods courses in the Normal School training, so that these graduates would be properly equipped to teach their Faith as well as secular subjects, she learned that many of the boys would not go to confession because they had been told by their elders—some of whom belonged to the Aglipayan sect—that the priests gave unheard-of penances. She prevailed on one of the boys to meet Father for just a talk, and the youngster was soon persuaded that there

was nothing eerie about the priest. Once he had gone to confession, he broke down the prejudice of the others in short order.

The Sisters' second retreat was a good deal more peaceful than the first, although it started with a "bang." They had assembled for the first conference, and the Jesuit Father was intoning the "Veni Sancte Spiritus," when from across the plaza a vigorous band struck up "Hail, hail the gang's all here."

Hawaii

Meanwhile a new mission venture was taking place in Hawaii, the crossroads of the Pacific.

Maryknoll's Father Kress had invited the Sisters to staff his new school in Sacred Heart parish in Honolulu. The Sisters arrived in September, 1927. Four days later the grade school opened with 93 boys and 77 girls. Sister Veronica was mission superior, and with her were Sisters Berchmans, Immaculata, Matthias, Robert, and Tarcisius.

The Sisters lived in the parish hall for three

years under unbelievably inconvenient conditions. When Mother Mary Joseph visited in 1928, she was given the privileged sleeping spot on the stage. "It was an odd sensation," she recalled, "to look up at the rafters through rolls of scenery, wondering just where you would find yourself if the curtain fell."

In the school itself there were a variety of difficulties to overcome. The children often came from homes where they received no Christian example and little encouragement to be good. Then too, a battle raged to get the students to speak English instead of pidgin, a local linguistic conglomeration. This battle has gradually subsided through the years.

Besides their unusual convent, they found an ideological difficulty to cope with in this parish.

This was to assist the pastor in persuading the people that Sacred Heart should be everyone's parish. Up to then it had been for "haoles," which on the islands indicates non-Portuguese white men.

The following year the Sisters took over a school and children's home on the Island of Maui. At the Maui school the students were mostly Portuguese at first, with a few non-Christian Japanese and a very few Filipinos. At the overcrowded home, on the same compound, there were a hundred children, boys and girls, ranging from infants to late teen-agers. In accordance with recommendations of the White House Conference of 1909, an effort was made to place these children with individual families whenever possible.

Punahou convent, surrounded by royal palms, was Maryknoll's first home in Hawaii. The convent was also known as "Termite Palace" and was literally on its last legs. In the background is the Sacred Heart School where the Sisters taught children of all the nations of the Orient, as well as Americans and Europeans.

While these mission efforts began and flourished, the congregation grew rapidly in the States, and the housing problem became acute. The Sisters still lived in eight frame houses on the Fathers' compound—some in St. Teresa's, some in Rosary House, others in St. Michael's, St. Joseph's, and Regina Coeli, and some even in two dormitories above the *Field Afar* offices. The professed Sisters had a chapel in Rosary House, so the novitiate could use St. Martha's Chapel. Both groups ate in St. Joseph's. One good snowstorm cut off all communications between various houses, leaving the whole community without Mass and most of them without a meal until the plows came through. Still, more and more women entered the novitiate every year.

The Congregation purchased a large farm across the street from the Fathers' property, and in 1930 building began on the new Motherhouse. It is a great rectangular building of yellow tapestry brick and brown tile roofs surrounding a cloistered garden. Except for the chapel and interior decorations, it was completed in time for the General Chapter of 1931 to hold its final meeting there. At this Chapter, the South China, Korea-Manchurian, Philippine, and Hawaiian regions were established, with Sisters Paul, Genevieve, Trinita, and Tarsicius as the respective regional superiors. It was also decided to make the Divine Office, which is the official prayer of the Church, the Community's prayer and to recite it in the vernacular.

Moving day was March 1, 1932. Mother Mary Joseph, her Council and Sister Felicita, the first Motherhouse superior, moved over a week earlier. All March 1st they packed, sorted, crated at one side of the road, and unpacked, unsorted, and uncrated at the other. The seminarians had a "free" day to help with the moving. Before they left the old compound, Father General blessed them and reminded them to thank God for His generous blessings and to pray gratefully for

Moving Day at last—March 1, 1932! Sisters from eight small, scattered houses moved into the big Motherhouse.

The Maryknoll Motherhouse—a dream come true—occupied in 1932.

Cleaning was the first job again—and in this huge house it was a major job for the eighty Sisters who moved in.

the many American families whose sacrifices in those hard depression days had made this new home possible. The next day there was a huge snowstorm, and there was nothing to do but stay in their new home and enjoy it. In the midst of their many delights they suffered the well-known but always unexpected calamity— the water power failed! Until they could arrange for an increased supply, even dishwashing had to be scheduled. Sister Felicita got so accustomed to reckoning gallons that when she called the local ice-cream dealer, she inadvertently ordered fifty gallons of ice cream! When he quoted the price, Sister was astonished and canceled the order, saying they could not afford it. Some time later the dealer called back to ask if Sister was sure she wanted fifty gallons! Sister laughed, explained her preoccupation with gallons, and then ordered fifty quarts of ice cream at a reasonable price.

Compared with the Fathers' compound, the Motherhouse grounds were a veritable wilderness. For many years only the barest work could be done on this, until during the war God brought good out of evil by having our Government release the interned Japanese rock and landscape artist Ryozo Kado. After his release, Mr. Kado and his family spent several years at Maryknoll, where his exquisite, patient, and detailed work, especially his masterpiece replica of the Lourdes grotto, has made the Sisters' grounds one of the beauty spots of Westchester County.

MANCHURIA

With all these goings-on at home, the missions still received first attention, and in the midst of building, new expenses, and the sharp growth in the Community, an invitation to work in another mission area was accepted. It was Manchuria, an area larger than Texas, to the north of Korea and northeast of China. This country, rich in mining and agriculture, had a population of 40 million.

In 1840 Manchuria was made a vicariate when there were only 2,000 Catholics scattered among the millions of non-Christians. By 1898 the vicariate was divided in two sections—north and south—each with a Catholic population about 15,000. A few years later, as a result of the Sino-Russian War, Russia relinquished her lease on Manchuria to Japan, and in 1915 China extended Japan's lease for 99 years. The Catholic populations continued to grow, and in 1923 there were 30,000 Catholics in the southern vicariate alone. Three years later, the Vicar Apostolic, Biship Blois, invited the Maryknoll Fathers to come, and Father Raymond Lane and Father Joseph McCormack were assigned. Father Lane, as superior of the mission, promptly put in his request for Maryknoll Sisters.

The Fathers had two parishes in Dairen, a city of 200,000 Chinese and 70,000 Japanese. Sacred Heart Parish served the Chinese Catholics, and Our Lady, Star of the Sea, the Japanese. The Sisters arrived in 1930. Sisters Eunice, Gemma, Angelica, and Coronata came from the States, and Sister Juliana from Hong Kong. In Japan they were joined by Unno San, a young Japanese woman from Tokyo. Upon arrival in Dairen she and Sister Gemma immediately started religion classes for the Japanese women and children.

Typically, they were plunged into the midst of things before they knew what was happening. Holy Week was upon them, and they were trying to make all things ready when they received word from Father McCormack in Fushun that Father Albert Murphy was critically ill and would the Sisters send a nurse. They did. Next they learned that Mother Mary Joseph was arriving for a look-see. In spite of their most hopeful efforts to prepare the convent for Mother's arrival, they were hampered by the fact that their furniture was coming on the same boat with Mother. Sister Columba and Sister Theodore accompanied her, and there was a grand reunion.

Dairen was a very modern, cosmopolitan city,

Lao Tai Tai shows the depth of Faith in Fushun, Manchuria, in 1934.

The peanut vendor. Life was hard but enjoyable in Manchuria in 1936.

*In Manchuria's bleak hills, a young Catholic
woman is laid to rest.*

rapidly developing under Japanese influence. Its trains were fast and prompt; its stores were filled with Western as well as Eastern goods; and it was here that the Sisters saw their first dial telephones. As a means of contact, English lessons were given to wives of Japanese businessmen.

On December 8, 1930, Sister Coronata made her final vows. Then she and Sister Eunice accompanied Father McCormack on their first mission trip to the outstations of Shan Cheng Tze and Erh Pa Tan. They traveled by train and "ma che" (mule-drawn cart), and at the first mission stayed overnight at the house of a fairly prosperous Christian who had been a bandit for thirty years before his conversion. He offered his property to Maryknoll at a nominal price in order to get a mission convent for his village as soon as possible. Erh Pa Tan, the second outpost, where Maryknoll's Father Leo Davis was pastor, was a predominantly Catholic village of four hundred to five hundred souls. Here they found seven young women, ranging in age from fourteen to twenty-one, who were anxious to become Religious, living at the mission in care of Bibiana.

"My mother died for the Faith. I want to live for it." This was Bibiana's ideal. During the anti-foreign Boxer Rebellion of 1900, Catholics were persecuted because their religion was considered foreign. Bibiana's father and mother were hurrying their children into the fields to hide, but her mother could not go on. She urged her husband to take the children to safety. The Boxers caught up with her and asked her if she was a Christian. She replied, "Yes." They went on to try to catch the family, but were unsuccessful, and returned. They asked the mother again, "Are you a Christian?" Again she answered that she was. Then the man began to strike her head with his sword. "Ai-yah, seng Mu!" (Oh, Blessed Mother) she cried out. Then, from her hiding place in the kaoliang (sorghum) field, Bibiana saw her mother's head drop off and roll on the ground.

Bibiana did everything she could in her own village to encourage the Faith. She devoted the greater part of her life to the Church as a catechist. It was she who directed the seven aspirants while awaiting the arrival of the Maryknoll Sisters. This was the nucleus of the Sacred Heart Congregation, recognized by the Holy See in 1940. First profession was on March 19, 1942.

At this village of Erh Pa Tan, the Sisters experienced their first Chinese breakfast banquet, during which many courses were served to the completely overwhelmed Americans!

In 1931 the Sisters opened the Maryknoll Academy—an elementary and high school in Dairen. Most of the pupils were Russians, whose families had left Russia upon the advent of Communism. Sisters Peter, Juliana, Famula, Coronata, and Ellen Mary were assigned. When finally all the permissions from the Japanese authorities and the Motherhouse at home were obtained, a suitable building located, the curriculum put in order, and an opening day set, the assigned teachers did not arrive. Opening day was postponed two weeks. True to the "latecomers' early start" tradition, the Sister-teachers arrived on Friday, and school began on Monday.

"It was bedlam!" was Sister Peter's succinct comment. Forty-one boys and girls ranging from five to fifteen years, mostly Russian, but with a few other nationalities intermingled, arrived for school. Not one of the pupils spoke English. Not one of the Sisters spoke anything else. Six years later, at their first high-school graduation, five children, all Russians, rated 100 percent in the math exams sent from Catholic University in the States, with which the school had become affiliated. The "bedlam" proved to be a teachers' paradise, for the children were eager students and scholarship was held in esteem.

Two weeks after the opening of the Academy in Dairen, four Sisters opened a mission convent in the large open-cut coal-mining city of Fushun. From Dairen they traveled on the South Manchurian Railway to Mukden. It was an all-day trip through endless fields of koaliang (sorghum) and soybeans. In Mukden they were met by Father Joseph McCormack who was Superior of all the territory in Manchuria that Rome had assigned to Maryknoll. With him they boarded a train for Fushun, thirty miles east of Mukden.

It was just three weeks earlier, on September 18, 1931, that outside the city of Mukden a bomb had been set off on the South Manchurian Railway. Japanese troops, alleging that the bomb had been placed by the Chinese, immediately seized Mukden, the government seat of Manchuria. This explosion, which blew up a part of the railway tracks, was the beginning of what the world calls the Manchurian Incident. It blew out of existence the Far East as the world had known it up to that time, and made obsolete every existing map of Asia. The Sino-Japanese undeclared war continued, and established Japan as a great continental power in the New Asia that Japanese armies proceeded to create. Manchuria was thus in a state of undeclared war when the Sisters opened their convent in Fushun. On October 9th, Sisters Eunice, Gloria, Veronica Marie, and de Lellis arrived, a few hours after two orphans and an aspirant for the soon-to-be-established novitiate had come.

The first meal and several thereafter were cooked and served by Father's "boy," Tu. But soon the Sisters decided to cook for themselves. The first day they started a fire in the stove and nearly burned the kitchen; the second day they filled the whole house with smoke from a clogged chimney; and the third day, just as the meat was done to a turn, the stove partially collapsed and the dinner went sliding onto the floor.

The Sisters' first two works were the orphanage with a school, and the novitiate. They began formal language study, and found that the orphan children were excellent and most patient teachers.

The aspirants for the novitiate came from Erh Pa Tan and Cha Kou, two Catholic villages. They brought with them their briar pipes, and were quite confused to find that the Maryknoll Sisters didn't smoke. Eventually they learned that their seminarian brothers had given up the custom of smoking, so they did too. Until their recognition by Rome in 1940, the aspirants concentrated principally on their education. They also assisted the Maryknoll Sisters in mission trips and catechetical instruction. This was one of six diocesan novitiates in which our Maryknoll Sisters trained local young women in the religious life. Besides this one in Manchuria and one in Korea, there were four in South China.

The long-range wisdom of founding purely native Sisterhoods was apparent in the troubled years of war and Communist occupation to come. When all Americans were repatriated from Manchuria and Korea during World War II, and expelled from South China in the early fifties, there were trained native Sisters ready to take over.

The Sisters soon extended their work to include a catechumenate and home visiting. Weekly the Sisters met with the lay catechists to discuss their activities and compare their methods and experiences. The pastor attended these conferences once a month, and weekly the Sisters visited each catechumenate.

On the feast of St. Joseph, 1932, the Sisters opened a dispensary, and because of the constant epidemics of flu, pneumonia, and smallpox, there were plenty of patients. One old man came to Sister Mercedes for help. On examination, Sister found that his feet were frozen beyond recovery. She gave him medicine and did what she could for him. In trying to get back into the rickshaw, the old man's foot was knocked off. He himself did not feel it, but the rickshaw driver cried out, "Ai-yah! Is that your foot!" Sister Mercedes hurried out, bandaged the stump, and helped the old gentleman into the rickshaw, instructing the fastidious driver to help him into his lodgings and promising to make a home visit to him the next day. When

In her "Little Tin House" clinic in Fushun, Sister Maria takes care of a little boy's infected leg.

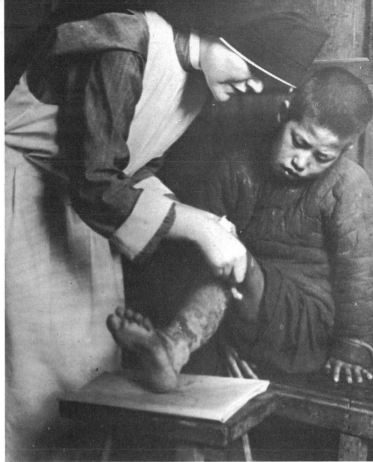

Sister Ellen Mary (below) playing with some of the orphans at Fushun.

she arrived she found the street outside the patient's lodging crowded with fascinated neighbors who had heard of the care and kindness of the "taifu" (doctor, as all the Sister-nurses were called). After attending her patient, she began to answer their questions, and a catechumenate was begun there and then.

Throughout the Manchurian missions everything that could not be bought locally was obtained by the excellent system of "can do." Show a seamstress a vestment, a carpenter a photo of a bed, and he or she would say "Can do," and in a very little time would reproduce the article perfectly. Lao Chang, "Mrs. Can Do," copied a cope in time to surprise Father Murrett with it at Christmas. Through her skill, an industrial department was begun that eventually provided work for twenty-five women.

The statue of Our Lady of Maryknoll, a gift of Bishop Lane in 1936 in memory of Father Founder, and now in the Motherhouse foyer, was carved at the Fushun Mission by a pagan, Lao Kuan. He allowed his children to be baptized during an illness, and as a result his wife decided to study the doctrine. She shortly became an enthusiastic Catholic, and won her husband to the Faith.

Although compared with the total population of Dairen, Catholics were still very few in number, their Faith was vividly meaningful to them, and they treasured it. Before the Maryknoll Fathers came, Mrs. Oka, who had been secretly baptized immediately after her own wedding, was an active apostle. She baptized dying infants, rounded up newly arrived Catholics from Japan for instructions, arranged for weekly prayer meetings, and did much else. Her son is now a priest, and superintendent of Catholic schools in Kyoto, Japan.

A Japanese girl, Yasuko San, who was converted after the Sisters arrived, was the beloved daughter of a Protestant minister. Her father did not object to her conversion, but his conscience about his own ministry would not allow him to keep a Catholic in his home. Heart-

broken, he brought her to the Sisters and asked them to care for her. She did not have the health to become a Religious, but she gave her life to God as a lay apostle, and served the missions as a catechist and in many other ways. When she was dying during the war, the Japanese permitted Maryknoll Father Edmund Ryan to leave internment to bring her the Last Sacraments. At her death, all the interned priests and Religious were allowed to attend her funeral.

The Chinese were not laggard in their devotion either. Lao Meng began taking English lessons with the Sisters, and eventually became a Catholic. But she could not persuade her husband to study the doctrine. He was always too busy. When he became ill he seemed more interested, and asked his wife to teach him about Jesus. The end was unexpected, and there was no time to get the priest. Lao Meng did what she could, and later hurried over to the convent to tell the Sisters what had happened.

"I think I baptized him," she said anxiously, "but I'm not sure."

"What did you do?" Sister asked.

"I poured water on his forehead and said, 'St. Joseph, I baptize you in the Name of the Father and of the Son and of the Holy Spirit.'"

Sister smiled a bit at this somewhat previous canonization, but assured Lao Meng that her husband had received the Sacrament. Then the battle began.

Lao Meng was determined that her Catholic husband would have a Catholic funeral. Her relatives, and especially his, had never heard of such a thing. A struggle of words and wills began that was resolved only when a Catholic layman was found to take over as master of ceremonies for the wake. He was able to satisfy the pagan relatives that all due respect was being paid the departed, while at the same time keeping out any practices that were openly superstitious. Sisters Luke and Jean attended the wake, and were nearly overcome when they found "St." Joseph laid out attired in hat, coat, glasses, and holding his rosary in gloved hands.

Sister Andre explaining holy pictures in a scrapbook to Korean children at Fushun.

However, their interest and presence were appreciated by the relations, and the storm over the funeral subsided. As the Sisters were leaving, Lao Meng mentioned to Sister Jean that it was just eight years since she had first wished to become a Catholic.

"Why, that's just when you started studying English with us," Sister commented.

"That," Lao Meng replied, "is why I started."

During the war when the priests, Brothers, and Sisters were interned, Lao Meng arranged for a committee of five Japanese and five Chinese Catholics to care for Catholic affairs in Dairen. She got permission from the Japanese for priests to be released from internment to go on sick calls. Since they were not released to say Mass, she traveled to Fushun, where she persuaded the Bishop to send a priest to offer Mass once a month.

The Dairen catechumenate brought some heartwarming stories to light. Two women began to attend a series of classes together, but it was not until they became eligible for baptism that the Sisters discovered that Chieh Chieh (Older Sister) and Mei Mei (Younger Sister)

Chang were wives of the same husband. Chieh Chieh could, of course, receive the Sacrament, but Mei Mei's position as second wife made this impossible for her.

As soon as Mrs. Chang received the Faith herself, she began a catechumenate in her own home, through which many of her relatives were converted, even Mei Mei's own mother. Still the younger woman could not be baptized, and she herself did not know how to solve her problem. Unexpectedly she became seriously ill, and was baptized in danger of death. However, she recovered, and now, having received the precious gift of Faith, she gave up her comfortable home and honorable position, and became a helper at the mission, eating with the other laywomen and sleeping on the "ovenbeds." She accompanied the Sisters on their mission trips, helping to spread her Faith.

Meanwhile Mrs. Chang adopted two of the orphans, and brought them up as her own. The good example of these two women, and undoubtedly the prayers and sacrifices of former Wife Number Two, brought Mr. Chang to the Faith shortly before his death.

MARYKNOLL

These and many other giant-hearted Christians etched for the Sisters Mother Mary Joseph's ideal—heroic generosity. Within the Community itself this spirit of joyful generosity was about to find a new outlet. Back in 1917 one of the newest members of the "Teresians" had confided to Mother Mary Joseph her growing desire for a cloistered, contemplative life and the conviction that God was calling her to it. Her happiness was beyond words when Mother in turn acknowledged that she herself desired to have as a hidden heart of her missionary Sisterhood a group of cloistered Sisters who would spend themselves with one heart and one soul for the same end as all other Maryknoll Sisters but whose specific work would be that of the contemplative apostolate. In 1917 this was a fair dream in the minds of Mother and her fifteenth religious daughter, who became Sister Mary Magdalen. Fifteen years were to pass before it became a reality. Sister Magdalen was among the first four sent to help the Pacific Coast Bishops with their Japanese parishioners in 1920. She was assigned after that to lead the pioneer group that began work in Bishop Ford's mission in Yeungkong, South China. When she was recalled to the Motherhouse in 1925, it was to be novice mistress for six years.

Sister David, in 1929, in the cannery under St. Joseph's, takes time off from the potatoes to dream of the missions. She has served seventeen years in Hawaii.

The novices didn't escape the setting-up-exercise fad of the early 1930's, but they enjoyed it along with all the other good and sometimes funny things the Lord bestowed upon them.

Two novices carry the "coffee break" to the office Sisters. Sister Colombiere, on the left, subsequently served nineteen years in China; Sister Colman, on the right, after sixteen years in the Philippines, is now the Congregation's Mother General. This picture was taken in 1927 or 1928.

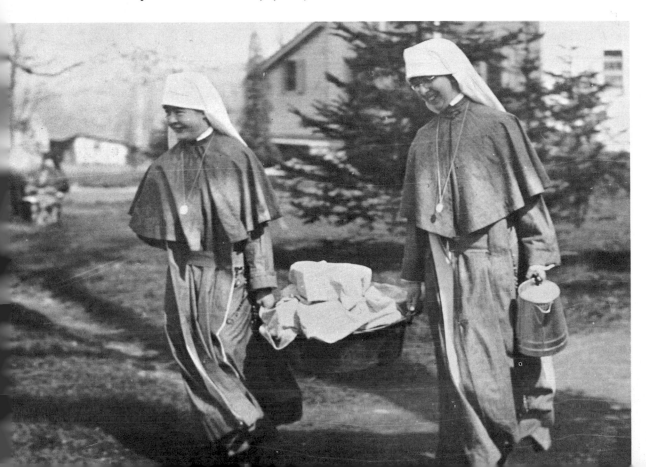

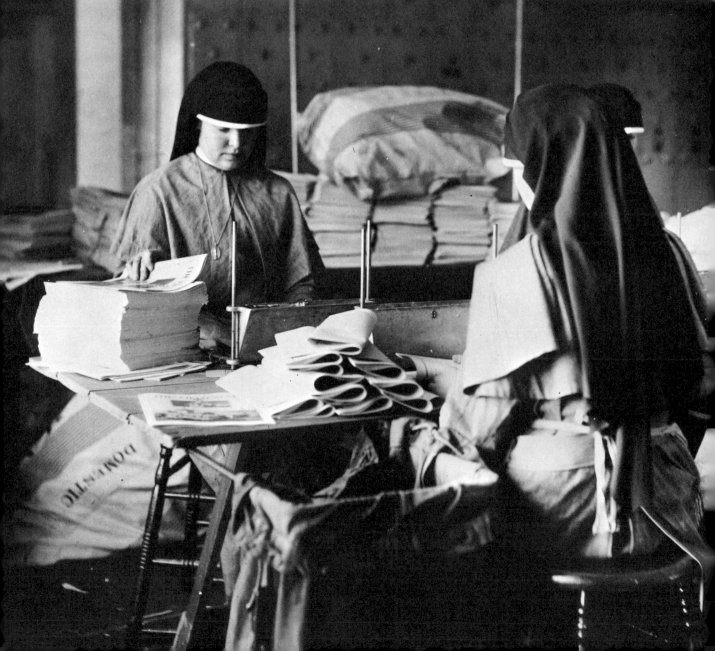

In 1931 the chair brigade (left) sometimes called the Maryknoll Movement, resulted from the Sisters having only one set of chairs, so that each took her own with her wherever she went, from chapel to refectory to work and to recreation.

(Below) *Every summer, just before the students arrived for the scholastic year, the Sisters literally scrubbed the seminary. This is in 1931.*

(Left) *In 1930 mailing* The Field Afar *was a monthly task that the Sisters went on shifts to get done.*

Spring cleaning in 1930 found Sister Esther Marie (right), *now in the Philippines, washing the windows in* The Field Afar *building.*

Departure-Day smiles, 1931. Left to right: Sister Grace bound for Hawaii, Sister Rose of Lima for Korea, Sister Anthony Marie for South China, and Sister Catherine Marie off to Hawaii.

In 1932 her dream was fulfilled. On the property where the Motherhouse was built, high up the hill was an old farmhouse that the Sisters re-named Regina Coeli and that had served for a while as one of their many "homes." When it was vacated, Mother decided it could become the Cloister. That year ten professed Sisters received their coveted assignments as cloistered missioners to represent the entire Congregation in a life dedicated to the praise and glory of God.

In 1931 Mother began another long-range project. She arranged for Sister Mary de Paul to begin a teacher-training school at the Motherhouse. Mother had always encouraged educational enrichment for all her Sisters and had provided various courses whenever opportunities arose. Now Maryknoll Teacher-Training School was set up with a three-year course. This was to develop in later years into Maryknoll Teachers College with a fully accredited four-year course leading to a Bachelor of Education degree. From the beginning it gave the Sisters an excellent secular education necessary for their work, interwoven with and enhanced by the depth and vitality of their spiritual training.

Meanwhile other communities that had colleges for laywomen were generous in providing additional opportunities for the Maryknoll Sisters to continue their studies. Every year several Sisters were assigned to study liberal arts or science at Mount St. Vincent's in New York, at Manhattanville, at Catholic University in Washington, or to train as nurses at Providence Hospital in Washington, D.C., and at Providence Hospital in Seattle.

The Motherhouse Chapel in 1933.

On snowy days in 1932 a team of farm horses pulled the sleigh carrying the Sisters to their work in the seminary kitchen or Field Afar *offices.*

Mother Mary Joseph (left), Christmas, 1932, at her desk in the Motherhouse. Mother was a good executive who used her time well, and therefore was never too busy to be interrupted.

In the late 1920's winter sports attracted the novices and got them out in the fresh air.

Winter makes Maryknoll a fairyland, but in the early days snow and ice made it very difficult to get from the Motherhouse to the work buildings on the Fathers' compound.

Sister Margaret Mary, the postmistress (left), kept the steps of her post office clear through wind and snow in the 1930's.

Sister Kathleen (right), *the choir director, taught Gregorian chant, with its unfamiliar notations, by using huge enlargements of the hymns and Mass texts. This is the "Salve Regina" sung at Compline.*

Gold-plating sacred vessels was one of the Congregation's works. Sister Chaminade (below) *puts the finishing touches on the base of a chalice.*

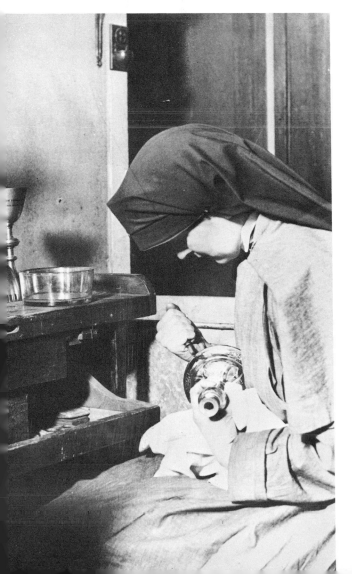

(Right) *A free day—perhaps Ascension Thurs-
day or the Fourth of July in 1934—and the
novices enjoy a picnic in the woods.*

*Noontime recreation period brought skating en-
thusiasts down to the pond for a half-hour of
refreshing fun.*

(Right) *Picnics involved a lot of work for the
generous kitchen staff, but a day outdoors was a
great treat for the Sisters. These are novices,
about 1933.*

Regina Coeli, the Maryknoll Sisters' Cloister (right), was opened in 1932 in an old farmhouse up the hill from the Motherhouse. A new cloister was built in 1960.

The "first ten" were photographed behind the grille shortly after the Cloister was opened in 1932.

(Right) *Even the original ten cloistered Sisters were crowded in the tiny oratory.*

75

CHINA IN THE LATE 1920'S AND 1930'S

Each area in the missions continued to expand. In China the Maryknollers had returned to Yeungkong for a relatively peaceful fourteen years. They learned to appreciate the Chinese qualities of respect and reverence for parents, devotion to family life and tradition, gracious hospitality to all, no matter how poor, the ability to relax in trying circumstances, and patience under suffering and injustice.

When Maryknoll took over the Kaying, South China, mission, Fathers Ford and Drought worked out a four-point mission policy that included the preparation of a Chinese Sisterhood and Direct Evangelization. Our Sisters shared in both these works. In 1933 four Maryknoll Sisters, with Sister Mary Dolores as Superior, left Hong Kong with a group of aspirants, who had been studying there under the direction of the Sisters, to set up a Chinese novitiate in the Kaying Prefecture. The following year six Sisters were chosen to launch a new apostolic venture. They rejoiced in the opportunity to put into action Bishop Ford's wonderful apostolate described by Sister Marcelline in *Sisters Carry the Gospel:*

"The Sisters were now going into the heart of China: to the market towns and surrounding farming villages, whose inhabitants sometimes were all one family. This was southern China; a land of rolling hills with sudden vaunting peaks; a land of wheat and rice fields, sometimes green, sometimes white for the harvest; a land of sturdy, pioneering people with strict morals, simplicity and love of home; a land strikingly similar in many ways to Palestine in which Christ preached the good news of His love. When, under Father Ford, they formally began their apostolate in these villages, the Sisters found their mission was primarily spiritual. The women had had no schooling but were wise in natural knowledge and had all the refinements of educated hearts.

"The markets, for instance," Sister Marcelline wrote, "must have been practically the same [as in Palestine], with their number of shops, resembling stalls, numbering from twenty to fifty to a hundred, close together and opening on a cobble-stone street or two, in a zig-zagging fashion, with no pretense at regularity. There were shops for the carpenter, the silversmith and the tinsmith, the tailor, and the potter; there were portable counters for the sale of thread and cloth that had been spun or woven at home; there was a public scribe on the corner, and a dealer in Chinese scrolls; many other small businesses, and vendors of unleavened cakes, fruits and vegetables.

"Then, the houses. They were made of mud and straw, some wood and stones from the hills; they had few windows, and in some rooms none at all—the door was used for light, and often in place of a chimney. Inside the house there were oil lamps, the water jugs, the cruets for oil and other earthen jugs, the scanty cooking utensils, the chest for valuables, the dirt floor and the house partitions; one section for the family and another for the buffalo, the goats, the ducks and the chickens.

"The neighborhood was awakened by the crowing of the cocks. The area had a well for general use where women drew water and carried it with a rhythmic step as they exchanged daily news; oxen or buffaloes were yoked to primitive plows, and the sowers went out to plant their seed; there was a common threshing square for the villages, and side doorways in the homes opened to the sight of a winnowing machine or a grinding stone."

The pioneers in this movement of evangelization were Sisters Imelda, Anna Mary, Rita Marie, Augusta, Madeleine Sophie, and Jean Theophane. Their activities included five years of part-time language study. They wrote papers on the Sisters' work, and these were discussed at the yearly reunions, which included a retreat given by Bishop Ford. At the reunion the policies, problems, and methods were reviewed and

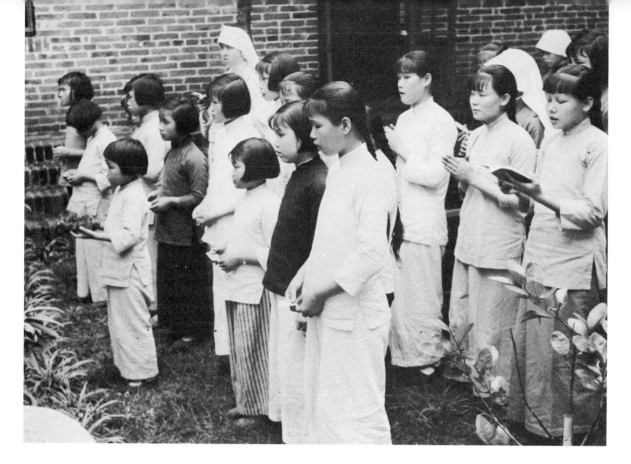

At Kongmoon aspirants gather with Sister Miriam Carmel at an outdoor shrine for night prayers. In several of their Chinese missions the Maryknoll Sisters trained girls to become religious in local diocesan Communities. The Sisters now have charge of such novitiates in Formosa, Africa, and Latin America.

Demand for the lightweight vestments grew, and the Hong Kong industrial room expanded rapidly during the 1930's, providing employment for and contact with many workingwomen. A good percentage of these women entered religious Communities in Hong Kong.

evaluated and plans made for the coming year. This training had far-reaching effects on mission work throughout the Chinese and Oriental mission areas. The Sisters lived in the villages they sought to evangelize, returning to a center house only bimonthly for a day of recollection. Bishop Ford placed major emphasis on the spiritual mission—"doing truth in Charity, preaching Christ, not their personal discolorations."

Sister Marcelline became Novice Mistress of the native Sisterhood after Sister Dolores broke her hip in 1935, and continued in this work for fifteen years until ousted by the Communists.

On September 21, 1935, Monsignor Ford returned to the States to be consecrated Bishop at Maryknoll. It was the last public ceremony in which the ailing Bishop James Anthony Walsh officiated. He was exhausted by it, but thrilled nevertheless that he himself had passed on the precious heritage of the full priesthood to his first son in Christ. Bishop Ford chose as his episcopal motto: To SUFFER WITH.

In Hong Kong the Sisters began to build the new Maryknoll Convent School, the cornerstone being laid on May 26, 1936, by Governor Andrew Caldecott. In Wuchow, to the northwest, they began another native novitiate. At the same time spiritual growth was encouraged through regular conferences and courses in Church history and Ascetical Theology.

MANCHURIA, LATE 1930'S

In Dairen, Manchuria, Sisters Veronica Marie and Mary de Lellis opened an elementary school, catechumenate, and a dispensary in the Chinese parish. These works were a part of every Manchurian mission where Maryknoll Sisters were stationed. Bishop James E. Walsh later called their Dairen Chinese mission "the most apostolic convent I have yet seen." Two aspirants from the native novitiate in Fushun, Pai Salome and Ding Malia, who later became Sister Herman, the first Mother General of the

In the Cloister garden, a Crucifixion group, donated by Bishop James Anthony Walsh, remains an enduring memorial to the beloved co-founder of Maryknoll.

Sacred Heart Sisters, helped them with the schoolwork. The story of one of the Manchurian dispensaries is etched for us by Sister Maria:

"The little tin house at one side of the Fushun compound is not a garage. It is our missionary dispensary. The cracks in the walls may be stuffed with newspapers to keep out the Manchurian breezes, but the treatment room contains the essentials: a white wooden table, a medicine cabinet, and two chairs. My native helper, Malia, is not able to read English, so we wrap aspirin in red paper, and other commonly used drugs in blue, green, or yellow paper. I call for drugs, not by name, but by color.

"Yesterday morning despite biting winds and sub-zero weather I found thirty-three patients waiting outside. A young man was in great pain and holding his hand in the air. A coal car had run over his hand in the mines. A friend had applied tooth powder to stop the hemorrhage, and now coal dust, tooth powder, bones, tendons and skin were all ground together. I clipped off two fingers, set the bones in the other three, and prayed while I was dressing it that the hand might be saved. I have to keep reminding myself that what we can do here for these poor people is better than anything else available for them in this area.

"Yesterday afternoon we visited a mud hut with a dirt floor to try to help the wife of one of our people. We found a paper shrine to a pagan god and the sick woman, her gums thick and black—typhus very obviously. Black spots indicated that it was too late to save her. She would die on the eighth day—tomorrow. While making her as comfortable as I could, I talked to her about God and heaven. In a short half-hour she asked to be baptized; someone's sacrifices somewhere had won a soul.

"On our way home a little boy ran up to us and asked if a day-old baby had a soul, because he knew where one was and it was dying. And so we baptized the dying infant. There are so many people here who need help!"

Later Sister Maria wrote home about the "Little Tin House," telling this story:

"It just happened to be a dull moment, so I called the two little girls who were looking in the window of the dispensary and said I would tell them a story. We talked about our guardian angels, and how they help us and what makes them happy and how much they love us. I was enjoying talking to them so much that I didn't notice Mrs. Chang come in. (She's been coming to the dispensary every day for treatment.) She's never so much as smiled at my little helper or me, and I was amazed to hear her ask me if there was a way she could make her heart clean, and who were these guardian angels we were talking about? Anyway, by the end of the visit, Mrs. Chang had asked to take catechism lessons.

"But the next day she announced very sadly that she could not become a Catholic because Mr. Chang, now fifty-three, was a builder of pagan shrines, and if he embraced the new religion he couldn't work. And she was sure our Spiritual Father wouldn't allow her to enter the Church alone. Three days ago Mrs. Chang walked into the clinic happier and brighter than I have ever seen her. Mr. Chang offered to teach her the catechism if she didn't try to coax him into becoming a Catholic too. But the first night he stayed up all night and read the entire catechism. The next morning after an absolutely silent breakfast, he announced that he was joining the Church. 'Heavenly Lord, help us! How will we eat?' Mrs. Chang exclaimed. But that morning a man at the city gate offered Mr. Chang a position where he could sit all day and write characters."

Sister Maria concluded the story in her letter by adding that she had visited the Chang home yesterday, and "in a corner of Mr. Chang's old workshop, already getting dusty, stands a unique tribute to his new-found happiness—an unfinished shrine to a pagan god."

The Maryknoll Sisters extended their work among the Japanese in Fushun, adapting their mission approach to the temperament and interests of these people, to whom they longed to

One of the older girls (left) of the Fushun orphanage finds wild flowers on a picnic in 1935.

A Catholic bride outside the Dairen church in 1936.

First Communion Day (above) at Fushun Mission, about 1936.

Sister Jean (right) with three of her kindergarten graduates outside the church in Dairen, Manchuria, in 1938.

The orphans at Fushun, Manchuria, in 1935,
were a continual source of delight to the Sisters.
Some liked cameras, some didn't. Some pre-
ferred St. Patrick.

bring the good news of Christ. As everywhere
in their Japanese missions, they began with a
kindergarten, for the devotion of the Japanese
parents to their children is renowned. The Sisters also visited the hospitals where they were
able to comfort the dying with the truth of
God's love.

Sister Andre came from ten years in Korea to
begin a mission for Fushun's Korean population.
This work began in 1937 just before the tragic
capture and subsequent murder of Maryknoll's
Father Jerry Donovan by the bandits. The Korean Catholic church was outside the walls of
the city, and considered unsafe after sunset, so
the little Korean community "borrowed" the
Japanese church for their Lenten evening devotions.

KOREA, LATE 1930'S

The missions in Korea expanded too. At Yeng You the Sisters began an embroidery department that eventually provided both work and education for forty girls. At Pyeng Yang, in a group of Korean-type mud huts, a native novitiate was begun. Maryknoll Sister Agneta Chang, after completing her studies at the College of the Sacred Heart in Tokyo, came here to be novice mistress of this group. Here, too, the Sisters worked with other nationalities, particularly the Japanese, for whom they started a kindergarten under the direction of Sister Bernadette, herself a Japanese.

Finally, in Shingishu began the medical work for which Maryknoll's mission in Korea became renowned. Sister Mercy, a doctor; Sister Rose of Lima, a pharmacist; and two or three Sisternurses pioneered this long apostolate. Sister Rose of Lima also managed to squeeze in time to train two outstanding choirs to sing the Mass and other religious services.

HAWAII, LATE 1930'S

Hawaii was already counted as a region. Four grade schools on the Island of Oahu and one on Maui flourished, and in 1935 Maryknoll High School was opened in Honolulu.

The schools expanded their activities in all possible ways. They began scouting, which was eventually taken over by laywomen. They had all the customary school activities. They took part in educational conferences. They attended the local university when they could afford to. They had a regular program of home visiting in which the Sister who had the eldest child of a family in her class visited the family.

The Sisters obtained an allowance from the Bishop for the Maui Children's home, through which they were able to make the building more attractive and homelike. They continued their efforts to place the children with families.

PHILIPPINES, LATE 1930'S

In the Baguio mountains of the Philippines, shortly after the opening of the convent in March, 1929, Sister Lucy began tutoring three children. Before the year was out, she was working with nine grammar-school and two high-school pupils. Within three years there were sixty students under instruction.

In 1936 the Malabon Normal School moved from Malabon to Manila, and was renamed Maryknoll College. The grade and high school continued at Malabon as St. James Academy. In 1938 another school was opened at Lucena.

SHANGHAI

A new work was undertaken in Shanghai, China's exotic port city. In 1935 Sir Joseph Lo Pa Hong, an outstanding Catholic, who called himself "The Coolie of St. Joseph," asked Mother Mary Joseph to send Sisters to take charge of a hospital that he had built for the mentally ill and that he supported for the most part himself.

Nine Sisters arrived and took charge of the women patients; the Brothers of Charity of Germany cared for the men. The patients ranged from Shanghai's poorest to a wealthy few. Many came from prisons where they had formerly been kept, and they still bore the marks of the chains that had restrained them.

In Heeia, a country parish in Hawaii, the children came early to help clean up for the opening of school. Life centered upon the church, convent, and school.

Junior High School Graduation at St. Anthony's, Kalihi, Honolulu, in 1937 (below) depicts the mixture of races among these citizens-to-be of the United States. The twenty-three youngsters here include Portuguese, Korean, Chinese, Hawaiian, Puerto Rican, Japanese, and "Haoli" (non-Portuguese white).

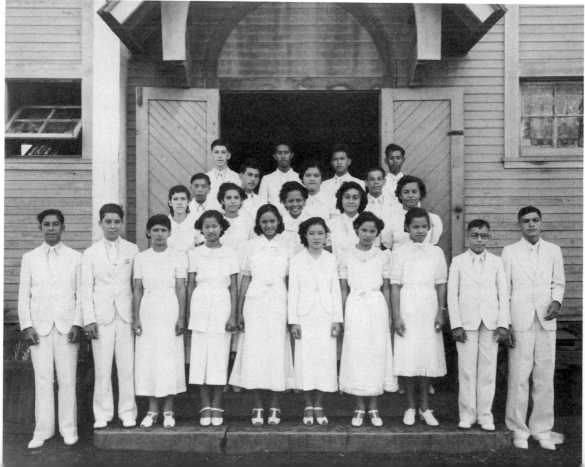

MARYKNOLL
NORMAL COLLEGE
COURSES RECOGNIZED BY GOVERNMENT

(Above) *Sister Agnes Imelda chats at the entrance to Maryknoll Normal College in Manila. The college first opened in Malabon, and moved to Manila in 1936, where it continued until evacuated during World War II.*

The schoolboys at Heeia didn't shirk work to keep their school grounds nice looking. There were always plenty of helpers to call upon among the Hawaiian youngsters.

On their first day there, three Dominican Fathers who were going through Shanghai stopped at the hospital, and each offered Mass. Next day the Sisters found many of their patients wandering up and down the halls with towels draped over their heads, alternately mumbling and intoning loudly. The daily attention and loving care that these people received was a vivid contrast to their previous isolation and neglect.

However, by 1937 China and Japan were at war, and the Japanese armies soon neared Shanghai. Sir Joseph Lo called together the staffs of the hospital and explained the danger, leaving those who wished, free to go. Most stayed until they experienced the first bombing. The Maryknoll Sisters continued, and in a while the hospital became a refuge for many who were fleeing the Japanese, including some disguised Chinese military men. At one point over twelve hundred people were crowded into the compound. Outside, the battle raged, and on November 9th, Shanghai fell. Two days later the hospital staff asked, and obtained, permission to bury the dead. Two Brothers and two Sisters buried six hundred bodies within the next few days.

The city was in desperate straits owing to the failure of water and electric power, and the Japanese asked Sir Joseph Lo to reorganize the plant.

Although he knew that many would consider it an act of collaboration, he agreed to do so, realizing the desperate plight of the poor of the city. The political and economic situation created bitter misunderstandings that inevitably led to violence, in the midst of which Sir Joseph was assassinated on December 30, 1937.

The Maryknoll Sisters continued work at the

An orphanage for little boys, another of the charities supported by "The Coolie of St. Joseph," who is in the rear wearing dark glasses. Sir Joseph Lo was assassinated by a misguided zealot after the fall of Shanghai.

In Shanghai, Mercy Hospital for the mentally ill was one of the many charities of Sir Joseph Lo Pa Hong, "The Coolie of St. Joseph." Shown here are the chapel and main entrance, with the men's pavilions on the right, the women's on the *left. The Maryknoll Sisters staffed this hospital for three years, during which time the battle of Shanghai was fought in 1937 between the Chinese and Japanese, and thousands took refuge on the hospital grounds.*

hospital as the Japanese occupied the city. Tension between Japan and the United States soon made their position very awkward. Besides, calls to open new missions and strengthen old ones came to Maryknoll every day; the Sisters were needed all over the world. At the same time, Franciscan Sisters from Germany were looking for just such work; their nationality would protect them and their patients in the event of a crisis. The Brothers of Charity in charge of the men's pavilions were also German. An exchange was made; and in 1938 Maryknoll Sisters withdrew from Mercy Hospital, and the German Franciscan Sisters replaced them. These courageous Brothers and Sisters continued on until ousted by Communists in 1951.

JAPAN

In 1935 Monsignor Patrick Byrne, then in charge of the Maryknoll work in Japan, asked for Maryknoll Sisters for Kyoto, which had been the site of the ancient capital of Japan from 794 to 1869. Sisters Rachel, Edward, Hostia, and Eleanor Francis arrived in the spring of 1937, and took up residence in a rented house near the place where Monsignor Byrne planned to have a sanitarium for tuberculosis patients, since the disease is prevalent among the Japanese. Japan in the summer of 1937 was already at war with China, and the necessary government permissions were slow in coming. In the meantime the Sisters began teaching English on the one hand and studying Japanese on the other.

A disaster to their mission world occurred when one morning their convent burned down from unknown causes, although defective electric wiring was suspected. Fire is a major hazard in Japan, where most of the houses are wooden. Only three Sisters were at home when Sister Eleanor Francis discovered the smoke in the rear of the building and ran to give the alarm. With superhuman strength they managed to remove the beautiful Oriental altar with the Blessed Sacrament. The police conducted a thorough questioning until 8:00 P.M., since, because of the hazards involved, carelessness is a serious offense. Later the Sisters learned that a kindly Japanese gentleman, though not a Christian, had taken on himself the duty of visiting each of their neighbors and apologizing for the fire and the danger caused them. He realized that the Sisters would not yet know enough of Japanese etiquette to do this for themselves. Monsignor Byrne arranged to have the priest and other students evacuate their language house at Karasaki, about ten miles away, and the Sisters repaired to that welcome haven late the same night.

HONG KONG

In Hong Kong, Maryknoll Convent School had grown in twelve years from a kindergarten for a dozen students to a grade and high school for five hundred. That year, all members of the first graduating class passed the Hong Kong University entrance exams, and one pupil won a four-year scholarship to the university.

But as the works flourished, the heavy foreboding of war began to hang over these mission lands. China was already in the grip of a struggle between Japan from without and Communists from within. The first mission to feel the burden of the terror to come was the hospital at Shanghai. For some missions, destruction was on the doorstep; for others there would be a few more years of peace and growth; but the privilege of sharing in the hard and good fight for freedom awaited all.

III

War and Recovery / 1938 *to* 1950

THE MISSIONS IN CHINA were the first to feel the effect of the war that was about to engulf the entire world. China and Japan had declared war against each other, and China herself was being undermined from within by Communists. This war raged across the great expanse of China, ebbing and flowing around the mission cities.

As early as the summer of 1937 there the Kaying area was bombed and strafed. During one of these raids Sisters Imelda and Rosalia were caught in the open. A Chinese woman risked her life to break off branches from a bush, and run out to the prostrate Sisters and hastily camouflage them.

Kweilin was made a prefecture in 1938, and three Sisters were assigned there to open a novitiate to train Chinese girls for the religious life. They also opened a clinic and did catechetical work. Eventually a Sister-doctor was assigned. The area was bombed constantly.

Mother Mary Joseph made her last Visitation to the Oriental missions in 1940, but was unable to reach the interior of China, nor could the Sisters get out to her.

Three from Kaying were forced to make the hazardous journey through Japanese lines to Hong Kong, when Sister Anna Mary became fa-

tally ill. It took another two weeks to get back into Kaying. The missioners were machine-gunned, strafed, and bombed daily. As they left one village, the house in which they had stayed overnight was destroyed by a direct hit. They could travel by sampan during the night only, and had to leave the boat early before the strafing planes arrived. One morning they had only reached the beach when the planes came. The two Sisters dropped prostrate into the shallow water as the bullets kicked up mud all around them—yet they were not touched.

The missions at Kweilin and Wuchow suffered similar hazards, yet the novitiates flourished and the village catechetical programs grew.

As the war tension tightened throughout 1940, the United States Consul advised the Sisters to evacuate all but a skeleton staff. After surveying their works, the Sisters decided that all they had was a skeleton staff, so they remained. They did so at their own risk.

The year 1941 dawned calmly. Mother Mary Joseph had returned to the States. Contact with the interior missions remained sporadic.

In Hong Kong, on December 8th, children came to school, since it was not a holy day in

The China missions in Kaying were not touched during World War II, and the work of teaching the young their Four R's flourished.

the Colony. Planes began to come over the city. Bombing began, and steadily increased. The news of Pearl Harbor raced through the city. Soon the Japanese infantry poured in, on foot, on mules, in trucks pulling heavy artillery. A contingent of soldiers took over the ground floor of Maryknoll School. The Sisters were confined to a section of the basement. Reluctant permission was given for Maryknoll Father Maurice Feeney to remain in the building, and thus the Blessed Sacrament could be reserved.

Hong Kong fell on Christmas Day, and twenty-three Maryknoll Sisters were forthwith interned as enemy aliens. The remaining five were non-enemy nationals. After two months three Sisters were released and joined these five. All eight then moved to Maryknoll Holy Spirit School. By September 12, 1942, all the Sisters were free with the exception of two. They volunteered to remain in camp to teach the women and children.

News from the interior was still scarce. Sisters Patricia and Beatrice had been ousted from Kongmoon and had gone to Portuguese Macao, fifty miles or so from Hong Kong. There they cared for several hundred orphans. Soon other Maryknollers came to their help.

On Christmas Eve, 1942, Sister Mary Paul received word that the Japanese would give exit permits to all Maryknollers to leave Hong Kong.

In January, Sister turned over the keys of the buildings to the Christian Brothers, and the Sisters began their exodus into the mainland of China by boat, sedan chair, bus, train, and on foot. A few went to Loting and Wuchow; most made it to Kweilin. The convent there, built for three, housed ten Maryknollers and seven refugee Sisters. They cooked, ate, and slept in shifts, often using tables and desks for beds.

The war years proved fruitful in spite of the constant relocation of missions and personnel. Many lay people came out of Hong Kong, including some of the Sisters' former students. Those who were Catholic gave their pagan neighbors an impressive example of Christian living. Many of the students who had previously hesitated to ask for baptism because of parental objections now came into the Church.

Kweilin, the Sisters' wartime center mission. was also an American Air Force Base, and therefore a favorite Japanese target. The air-raid shelters were caves outside the city, and there the entire population spent many daylight and nighttime hours.

At Yeungkong Mission, Kwangtung, China, "Old Glory" protected the missioners during the bombings and Japanese invasion, 1938 to 1941.

River travel in China was hazardous and slow. A trip like this (below) *could take weeks for Sister Magdalena to reach Kaying.*

Home visiting—a part of the direct apostolate—was often a source of joy and consolation to Sister Regina Marie (above).

In spite of these constant hazards, Sister Mary Paul decided to visit the missions of the region. She headed first for Kaying which had been isolated from the rest of the Community for three years. In this land of the Hakkas she found six flourishing direct-apostolate missions, as well as a novitiate for Chinese Sisters. Then at Wuchow, Loting, and Yeungkong, everywhere Sister found the mission work flourishing amidst physical destruction. Everywhere she found the Sisters experiencing God's special protection.

A demolition raid hit both mission and church at Wuchow, but no one was seriously hurt. Sister Chanel had moved from the back of the church, where the bomb hit, to the front, seconds before the blast. At Loting when the rectory was struck, Sister Monica Marie safely gave Maryknoll Father Robert Kennelly first aid out in the open with bombs dropping all around. "Well, Father," she said, continuing her medical administration, "your house is gone but the flag is still flying."

The Japanese advance gained momentum, and one by one the missions, except those in Kaying, had to be evacuated. Some of the Sisters returned to the States. Others wended their way across China as best they could. Five of them landed in Kunming, where they spent the rest of the war working for the Armed Forces, three as office workers and two as nurses in the Military Hospital. Four Sisters reached Chaotung, almost on India's border, and went to work in a Catholic Hospital run by Yugoslavian Sisters. Five others got into India and were assigned to various teaching posts.

All waited and wondered what was happening to their Maryknoll Sisters around the world. Their own bitterest suffering was yet to come.

The Rosary—a powerhouse around the world—is prayed by a Chinese grandmother (below) while her pride and joy contemplates the loving cross of Christ.

Hawaii

When the Japanese struck Pearl Harbor on December 7, 1941, all Hawaii, but particularly Honolulu, was caught up in the war in an instant. When the Islands had recovered from the initial shock, there was some uncertainty whether or not this was a prelude to invasion. But the enemy had succeeded in its objective—to cripple the fleet in the Pacific. War protection measures were enforced. Gas masks were issued to the population. Air-raid trenches were dug swiftly wherever necessary. The Sisters' school grounds were furrowed with them. The school yards became victory gardens. There were, by this time, six Maryknoll convents in Hawaii—four schools on the Island of Oahu, and a school and children's home on Maui.

Hawaii was a great base for all the Armed Forces during the war. On Maui a group of Marines, when off duty, began to come to the children's home in small contingents, to do necessary repairs, repainting, and whatever they could. They were not at all averse to Sister Daniel's doughnuts and cookies, when rationing

Like children everywhere, in 1947 the little Chinese were fascinated by Sister Maria Petra's medal and rosaries.

Non-Catholic Chinese girls (below) *at Hong Kong Holy Spirit School adopted the custom of visiting the Blessed Sacrament briefly between classes.*

would permit her to bake. Their work "boss" at Maryknoll was Sister Jeanette Nishimuta, a Japanese-American, to whose direction they cheerfully dedicated their abounding energies. They called themselves the Maryknoll Marines, and after the war, when Mother Mary Joseph visited the Islands, they insisted—much to her delight—on taking her for a ride around the harbor on an amphibious truck, from which she and they returned soaking wet but happy. Their generosity and friendliness delighted both children and Sisters.

On January 20, 1943, the Sisters took charge of Catholic Charities, the social-service department of the Church in Hawaii. The first "office" was a cubicle between the rectory and the church, occupied by Sister Victoria Francis, and jammed to the rafters with documents, case histories, current work, letters, and files. A steady stream of servicemen, intrigued by the constant activity and the tight quarters, dropped in on their way in and out of church to find out what was going on. This small but hectic opera-

Gas masks were the order of the day in Hawaii after Pearl Harbor was bombed on December 7, 1941. The youngsters are students at Maryknoll School in Honolulu.

tion was the tiny nucleus of a burgeoning new area of activity for the Sisters, who now have qualified Sister social workers in Hawaii, Hong Kong, Korea, South America, and on the United States mainland.

THE PHILIPPINES

In the Philippines the Sisters' work was flourishing. No one was seriously aware of the imminent danger until the Japanese struck Pearl Harbor, and immediately began their invasion of the Philippines.

Throughout December, 1941, the tension and difficulties mounted. St. Paul's Hospital was transferred by the United States Army to the Philippine Women's University buildings. Most of the Maryknoll Sisters gathered there. Many of their college and nursing students were still with them, as well as two Holy Cross Sisters, stranded in Manila on their way to India. The Sister-nurses had work aplenty and the Sister-teachers did the cooking, cleaning, clerical work, and practical nursing. Every day at noon and often at night there were air raids.

On Christmas Day Manila was declared an open city and the United States and Filipino armies withdrew to Bataan and Corregidor, taking the wounded with them. The air raids continued. The Japanese arrived on January 2, 1942. By January 11th the Sisters were advised they must get out of their building. They as-

A group of Leathernecks dubbed themselves the Maryknoll Marines, and came in small details during their free time to do repair and paint jobs here at St. Ann's on Oahu, and often to entertain the little ones at the Maui Children's Home.

sumed that this meant those students who were still with them should leave as soon as possible, and some of them did so. Through a misunderstanding the guards became excited about their departure and sent for reinforcements. The whole building was overrun by soldiers carrying hand grenades and bayonets. Sisters Bridgettine and Isabel were lined up before machine guns, and all the Sisters were ordered to remain where they were in view of the mounted machine guns. When Sister Georgea went to call the Jesuit College, a soldier dashed the phone from her hand. Finally a Japanese colonel arrived with a Protestant minister as interpreter, and the matter was cleared up.

The next day the Sisters were welcomed with the greatest kindness and generosity by Mother Rose, Superior of the French Assumption Sisters, at whose college they were interned until July 8, 1944. For a while there was no news of the Sisters at Baguio. By May, 1942, most of them were brought to Manila and interned at Assumption College with the others. In Manila, Sisters Concepcion and Claver, who were Filipinos, were still free to go out.

The internees set up a program of classes and work for themselves that kept them quite busy. The Sister-nurses worked again at St. Paul's Hospital. Sisters Colman and Miriam Thomas wrote their Ph.D. dissertations.

The years 1942 and 1943 brought a growing scarcity of rations, and an equally growing generosity on the part of the Assumption Sisters and loyal Filipinos alike. The help given by the Filipinos inevitably involved the risk of their own lives and welfare.

MANCHURIA

The Manchurian missions close to the fighting in China had felt the strain of war since 1939. Mission trips were restricted, and the consul advised those Sisters whose work was curtailed to leave the Orient. Only a very few were recalled, however.

How to keep house was part of the home training given the children at Maui Children's Home. Sister Agnese helps a youngster get her doll's dress into shape.

The mission work continued—Sister Marcus Marie takes time out from the laundry detail to explain the crucifix to a Chinese boy from next door.

The internment in Dairen is told by Sister Peter:

"Just before Mass on the morning of December 8 we learned of the attack on Pearl Harbor. For a while everything remained calm. We used every spare minute thinning out files and preparing personal belongings. News came in, mostly through our school children, of the internment of civilians—American, British, Dutch, Belgian, Hungarian. They were being held at a very good hotel.

"Just as we finished breakfast on December 12, about twelve policemen came into the compound. They went first to the rectory and within the hour came to our front door with Father Edmond Ryan and Brother Benedict. They told us we were to be interned, and they wished to go through the house.

"Two of the police went through every room, every cupboard, every desk, and every drawer. Cameras were picked up immediately. While this was going on Sisters from the Chinese Mission and from the Academy arrived under guard. With them were Father Leo Hewitt and Father John Lenahan. Each brought some luggage with her, and we were all greatly relieved—and showed it—to be interned in one house together.

"When I took Father Lenahan's overcoat he murmured: 'The Blessed Sacrament is in the pocket, Sister.' We hung the coat on a cell door, and made an act of adoration each time we passed it.

"Police guards were formally installed on the first floor and we were ordered to the second floor. On one side of the stairway the three priests and Brother Benedict established themselves in what had been two classrooms. We eleven American Sisters set up in the four small bedrooms and turned the small Community room into a dormitory for three. An eight by fifteen foot hallway was converted into a Community and work room.

"Sister Sabina, who is Japanese, was the only Sister left at the Academy. She and Furuya San, a young Catholic widow, stayed on together at the Academy Convent.

"The police rang the rising bell at 6:30 AM, roll call was at 6:55, then single file with the guard we went to church where the three priests offered Mass at the same time. When the hour we were allowed for prayers was up, the guard clicked his heels in the center aisle and announced: 'Time up.' We filed back to the convent and had our breakfast in the former kindergarten while the guards enjoyed a cup of coffee in the same room.

"In January the police began a series of investigations which proved extremely trying because of the nature of the questions asked. Each Sister was called separately. The first day it was Sister Gerard and I. The detective asked where our rooms were, told us to go to them, and came with us. I told him I didn't like the idea of being interviewed alone in my room and asked him to go to a public room—and to explain to his fellow-officer who was to interview Sister Gerard. He showed me his detective badge and said: 'No matter what I am in private life, when I am on duty I do no wrong.' However, he got up and knocked at the other room, and explained nicely. After that all these interviews were held in the Community room.

"They lasted three and four hours at a stretch in four or five sessions for each Sister—sometimes one day following another, sometimes at an interval of a week. The whole thing was intensely nerve racking. As each one finished, the questioner read a summary and asked if it agreed with what we had told him and then asked us to sign the paper.

"To my amazement and edification, when all was finished, the detective recalled our first interview, and apologized for having offended against our accepted etiquette. He said to believe him sincerely when he told me that from the bottom of his heart he admired our form of life.

"Nearly a year went by in this way. The government issued permits for us to have visitors on Mondays. Many came and brought gifts of food. Sister Talitha, a Japanese, came from Korea—where all the American Maryknoll Sisters were living in one convent at Yeng You— and joined Sister Sabina at the Academy. With her arrival and the help of former pupils, Helen and Sophia Kozlenko, and Joseph Lerner, classes at the Academy were resumed. In April 1942 Sister Marie Elise, who held a German passport, was released from Fushun and allowed to join the Academy Sisters.

"In mid-summer we were told we were to leave. September 1 was the day. We sang Mass that morning. Word of our departure spread and the people came and filled the back of the church, and were not told to leave. Up to that time the police had forbidden the people to come in to church if we were there. Sisters Sabina, Talitha and Marie Elise remained in Dairen. As Sister Sabina kissed me goodbye, she whispered: 'Don't let them forget us. We are Maryknollers, Sister.'

"The taxi procession to the wharf was like a funeral, and no one tried to speak. Our people from all the missions were gathered at the wharf to *see* us at least. When they were not chased away by the guards, they came closer, patted our arms and spoke briefly. The Japanese guards just turned their backs. At that the people closed in about us, and talked their hearts out. The whole departure was an unforgettable demonstration of the deep affection between them and us."

The internment at Fushun is related by Sister Lelia:

"It was a beautiful day—that December 8— and crowds attended High Mass. Then Father William Pheur brought the news of the declaration of war. Throughout the day the Christians brought word of anti-American posters being put up at various points, but all was comparatively quiet.

"Later that evening we confronted a little man in foreign clothes, felt hat pulled well over his eyes, in our compound. We slowly but surely advanced on him, and succeeded in piloting the unwelcome visitor out of the yard and into the open space at the front of the church.

"There to our surprise we found a whole military guard (Japanese and Manchu) in heavy overcoats and tall fur-lined caps. The Manchu officer told us not to worry about anything but to go to bed. Instead we went to the second floor from where we could see figures moving about the rectory and the priests—wearing hats and overcoats—among the men in uniform.

"About 8:30 PM Sisters Celine Marie and Veronica Marie started out for the Novitiate building. Sister Rita Clare and I accompanied them to the front door. Bishop Lane was at the compound gate and called out: 'Sister Lelia, they want us to take a look at the inside of the jail. I'll try to get back in the morning.'

"We moved down to the main mission gate. An army truck was waiting, with about thirty soldiers to take into custody six American priests and one Chinese—poor old sick Father Martin Pai.

"There was no sleep for anyone that night at the convent. About midnight came a peal of our front doorbell. We answered it—all together. It was only one of the Fathers' houseboys who said the visitors had gone but would be back in the morning to get us. He advised us to get ready for jail!

"Never having been in jail, especially a Manchu jail, we didn't know exactly how to get ready. We decided to wear all the warm clothing we could possibly put on. By four o'clock on the morning of December 9th, we were ready—each one having rested for a longer or shorter interval.

"When the Fathers did not return, I went to the rectory, and following Bishop Lane's earlier directions, with my woolen shawl for humeral veil, carried the ciborium to the big church where the congregation was waiting. I opened the main tabernacle and distributed Holy Communion to all who came to the altar rail—many of the good old faithful women with tears streaming down their cheeks. Significantly and characteristically of a Chinese congregation, not one man approached the altar rail. Though fervent and reverent, they were not prepared for such an innovation. I then went to the Novitiate and distributed Communion to the 18 Novices and Postulants and the remaining Maryknoll Sisters.

"All day of the 9th we waited and it seemed that the 'powers that be' had forgotten all about us. Bishop Lane and the Fathers were brought back to the rectory that night.

"December 10th a squad of military arrived in the forenoon, inspected the convent quarters —and laid down the law, telling us just how far we could walk around our own grounds and forbidding any communication whatsoever with the Fathers who were under military guard. Then they withdrew.

"Fearlessly, our good Christians, principally the elder women who themselves felt sure that no one would suspect them, carried information to Bishop Gaspaid, Apostolic Delegate in Hsin Ching, the capital, and to Bishop Blois at Mukden, and to several missions. Later Bishop Blois, who literally adopted our whole vicariate and sent a Chinese priest to offer Mass once a month, publicly paid tribute to the courage of the Fushun Christians.

"Christmas was a quiet one, with only one morning Mass for the parish. Bishop Lane celebrated his three Masses in the rectory dining room directly across the compound so that his Maryknoll daughters could at least watch.

"The school, the dispensary, the Mission Arts workshop were all closed. The Novitiate had been transferred to Mukden. We had to be careful not to be seen talking to·too many of our Christians at one time.

"Our washerwoman was turned away at the gate one morning by a guard, who told her to stop working for those foreigners. She waited an hour for him to go, and then came to work.

"Father Martin Pai never recovered from the exposure of the ride in the truck, and died on January 24th. Just six years later his brother, Father Maurus Pai, was publicly martyred for the Faith by the Communists."

In April the Sisters learned that eight of them were to be repatriated in May. They arrived home in the States on August 25, 1942. Several of them were to be out to new missions again before a year had passed.

The remaining five were not released until 1943. When the ship they sailed in reached Goa, they had the great joy of being reunited with three of the Sisters from Japan—Sisters Gemma, Dolorita, and Camilla—and of hearing how the mission there fared.

JAPAN

The tension in Japan had been evident for several years. On October 13, 1940, Monsignor Patrick Byrne turned over jurisdiction of the Kyoto Prefecture to Japanese Father Furuya, later Bishop of Kyoto diocese.

Sisters Edward and Hostia returned to the States. That left Sisters Dolorita and Camilla in Kyoto, and Sisters Gemma and Rose Ann, the latter a Japanese, in Tokyo, where they had the small beginning of a native Community.

In May, 1941, the Japanese Government made a proclamation recognizing the Catholic Faith as one of the approved religions in Japan. In view of the heroic persecution suffered by Japanese Catholics for hundreds of years, and their steadfast loyalty to the Faith through centuries when they had neither priests nor Sacraments, this was indeed a happy day. In July the Kyoto Sisters began a hostel for young women students.

War came on December 8th. The next day two detectives called and told the Sisters that they could continue to run the hostel provided they themselves did not go off the premises. They agreed.

In Tokyo Sister Gemma was interned when the war began. Sister Rose Ann went to Dairen to join the other Oriental Sisters in running the Academy.

On September 14, 1943, the three internees, Sisters Gemma, Dolorita, and Camilla, boarded ship and reached home with the Sisters from Manchuria, on December 1, 1943. Some of their co-missioners from the Orient had already departed for the new mission territories in Central and South America.

Latin America

With the war still raging and the missions closed in the Philippines, Japan, Korea, and Manchuria, and imperiled in China, the exiled Maryknoll Sisters responded wholeheartedly to a new call from a completely different area of the world. Latin Americans are Catholics—90 per cent of the people, Spanish and Indian alike, are baptized.

The Maryknoll Sisters went in 1943 to Bolivia, Panama, and to the Canal Zone. In 1944 they went to Nicaragua. The history of each South and Central American nation is individual, but there are many sufferings that the majority of the people throughout the hemisphere have experienced: the impoverishment of the working people, the hopelessness of getting out of debt; the illiteracy of most people due both to meager educational facilities and to the inability to spare children from work for school; the enervation brought about by both climate and disease; the loss of their natural wealth to foreign business enterprises. The people were Catholics, and they expressed the emotional richness of their Faith in devotions and processions that honored the mysteries of the life of Christ. However, since they had neither teachers to explain nor priests to administer the Mass and the Sacraments, they seldom shared in the very heart of Christianity.

Panama

Mother Mary Joseph announced in March, 1943, that Maryknoll Sisters would take a mission in the Canal Zone. The three Sisters assigned, who left that November, were Sister Lelia from Man-

churia, Sister Socorro Maria from the Philippines, and Sister Concepta Marie.

At once they began catechetical work and the hospital visiting that continues to this day. The catechetical classes began in various sections, usually among the very poor Jamaicans and West Indians brought in to work on the Panama Canal. Sometimes their little town settlements would be abandoned overnight as they, with their children, moved to another job, and that would be the end of the catechetics too, of course.

Several kindergartens begun in these shanty townships flourished and faded the same way and for the same reason. However, while they lasted they gave the Sisters the opportunity of contacting children and parents alike in the name of Christ.

Hospital visiting included the Gorgas Hospital and the Leprosarium. The Sisters' visits were eagerly anticipated. They brought literature in Spanish and English. Christmas, Epiphany, and Mardi Gras were the major celebrations at the Leprosarium, and the Sisters did everything they could to enhance these festivities. They begged money through letters and newspapers for a Christmas collection, and then, with a list for each patient, shopped for the entire hospital.

In Panama the Sisters assisted in the distribution of goods the Vincentian Fathers collected or bought for the poor. Every week the Fathers assembled one hundred pounds of rice, one hundred pounds of navy beans, a collection of canned goods in dented cans bought at a reduction, and sometimes clothing, medicine, and money. The Sisters packaged and distributed the goods in family-sized amounts, and kept track of the needs of the people who received them—sometimes a job, sometimes money for medical attention.

The people were mainly from a section in Ancon called "Hollywood"—where five hundred squatters lived in makeshift shelters. Others walked great distances for the needed help.

In 1944 the Sisters took charge of the school

Panamanian tough guy with a tin hat and a whistle never suspected that he might be teacher's pet.

Sister Francis Christine (left) gets rapt attention from this kindergarten class in Panama when she introduces Our Lady.

Sister Joan Muriel (right) taught a kindergarten in Chorillo section of Panama City, one of several opened by the Sisters for children of men working on the canal.

The Maryknoll Sisters staffed St. Vincent's School in Panama City for such wide-eyed, openhearted youngsters as this boy (right).

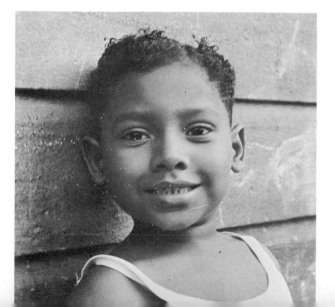

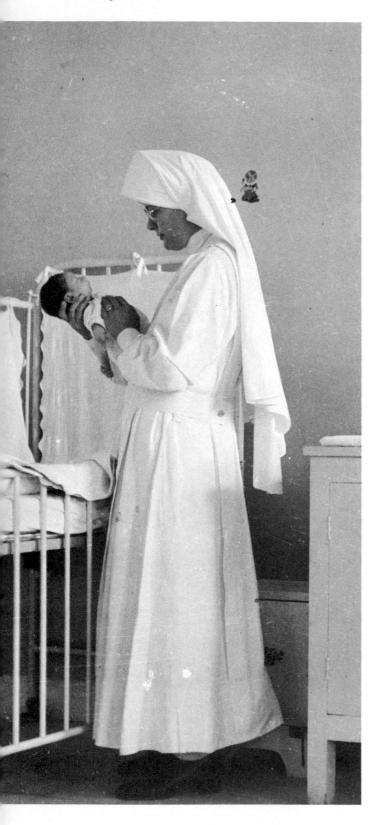

Sister Marie Marquette (left) *in the Riberalta Hospital inspects a brand-new Bolivian. Infant mortality has declined sharply in the years since the hospital opened.*

of St. Vincent in Panama City, where for twenty-two years a staff of lay teachers had held the fort as best they could. Because there were 150 children, in four grades, and only the parish hall for use as a classroom, the blackboards formed the partitions. The children were mostly from the English-speaking Negro families who had come from the West Indies to work on the Canal. As these workers decided to make Panama their permanent home, they began transferring their children to the government schools where the subjects were taught in Spanish. At the same time the Panamanians decided to give their children the advantage of English, and started sending them to St. Vincent's.

BOLIVIA

The Maryknoll Fathers were entrusted by Rome with the Pando Vicariate in Bolivia in 1942. They requested Maryknoll Sisters, and in the following year Sisters Mercy, Paula, Kateri, and Magdalen Mary arrived to do medical and educational work. Their "taxi" at the airport was an oxcart.

Bolivia was materially, religiously, and culturally very poor; 85 per cent of the population could neither read nor write.

The Sisters' work began at Riberalta, a town of eleven thousand on the Beni River, and at Cobija, capital of the Pando district on the Brazilian border. They found the Bolivians kind, friendly, innately courteous and immeasurably hospitable, as well as very practical but easygoing. The Bolivians admired but did not wish to imitate the organizational drive of the "gringos." The Sisters had two major mission aims:

Schools in Bolivia's jungle lands help to lower the 68-per-cent illiteracy rate. Sister Ann Catherine teaches the ABC's.

to combat ignorance of the Faith and to establish an atmosphere of living, practicing Catholicism.

The only transportation into this area was by riverboat or plane. The people were part Spanish, part Indian, mostly farmers and very poor, raising an inadequate diet of rice and yuca, with very few vegetables and little meat. They lived in adobe huts with palm-thatched roofs, and dirt floors shared with their livestock.

In addition to extensive catechetical, dispensary, and home-visiting work, the Sisters undertook the administration of a twenty-five-bed government hospital in Riberalta. Here, too, the first parochial school in all Bolivia was opened by the Sisters in 1945.

Although small, the hospital at Riberalta, Bolivia, is equipped for surgical work. Dr. Vaca Diez operating, Sister Mercy assisting.

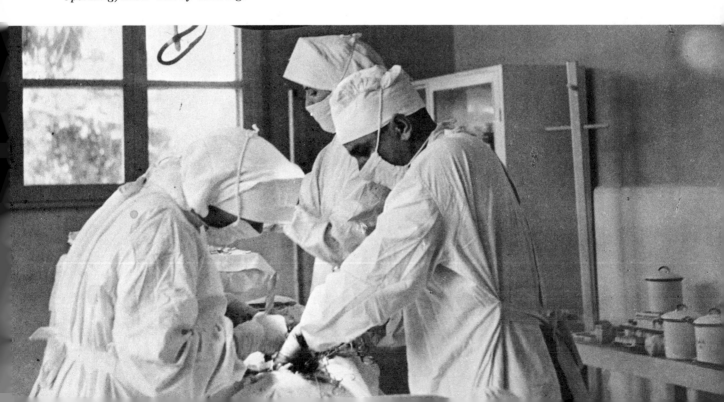

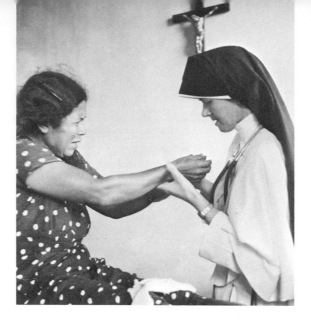

Sister Vivian, M.D., at work in the clinic and making home visits. With this week's wash on their heads and next week's in bundles, Sister's ex-patients enjoy a good chat on the street.

(Right) General Enrique Peñaranda, then President of Bolivia, came to the Motherhouse in 1943 to emphasize Bolivia's need for Maryknoll Sisters.

Sister Madeline Maria makes friends with a little girl in Riberalta while on a home visit.

In 1943 Christmas brought real rejoicing to the people of Cobija, for two days earlier two Maryknoll Sisters from Riberalta—Sister Magdalen Mary and Sister Paula, a teacher and a nurse—had at last come to live in their midst.

During the first month Sister Paula handled 388 sick calls. Sister Magdalen Mary, on one of her first mission trips, stopped at a farmhouse where a little girl, who had never before seen a Sister, looked at her and said suddenly, "That's

It was September, 1944, before the assigned Sisters could depart, owing to wartime travel restrictions. When they reached Managua, the Nicaraguan capital on the Pacific Coast, they learned their convent in Siuna was not ready for them. They were instead welcomed by the Assumption Sisters, the very Community that had at the other side of the world protected and cherished their Sisters in the Philippines during the war years.

what I want to be when I grow up." Ten years later the girl entered a religious Community in Brazil.

NICARAGUA

On June 29, 1943, American Capuchin Father Matthew Niedhammer was consecrated Bishop by Bishop James E. Walsh of Maryknoll, who shortly after persuaded the new Bishop to ask for our Sisters to help him in his new Vicariate of Bluefields, Nicaragua. Bishop Niedhammer spoke to Mother Mary Joseph of his poverty-stricken flock, and she promised him six Sisters, including one nurse, as a "consecration gift."

On December 24th the six Maryknollers left Managua in a small commercial plane and flew over the thick jungle to their new home. The townspeople were out full of enthusiasm to welcome them. They had leveled the ground for the convent and put up the frame themselves. They had built a new road leading to the Sisters' house and named it Boulevard Maryknoll. They cried out, "Viva las Madres de Maryknoll!" and the Madres assured them their hearts had been here with them long before they themselves arrived.

In the time before school was to open, the Madres studied Spanish and visited their new neighbors. The Nicaraguans are a mixture of Spanish, Indian, and Negro from the West

Two little rascals who may one day be priests. Nicaragua, with only one priest for 4,800 Catholics, needs them.

Indies. In this part of the country they worked mainly in a nearby gold mine. They were extremely poor, lived in dirt-floored thatched huts, and suffered from malnutrition, worms, malaria, and all the diseases that come with lack of sanitation.

The Clinic opened at once, and within three months Sister-nurse had treated over six hundred patients. In a little while the number rose to five hundred monthly. Work began at once on Nicaragua's first parochial school to serve the two towns of La Luz and Siuna.

When registration began, the mothers lined up at 6:30 A.M. Four classes were opened and 280 registered, including 168 for first grade. They were the lucky ones who had desks; at least they shared a desk, two and two. The upper grades sat on wooden benches that had been built early the very morning school opened.

The workmen sawed and hammered and the children listened with awe-filled attention to the Madres' still-hesitant Spanish—in which all the subjects were taught.

The mission of Siuna was on its way. The aims were to build strong Catholic families and to raise the standard of living. The growth and success of these new missions in South and Central America were undoubtedly supported by the keen suffering being endured by Maryknollers in the Philippines.

Humberto and his pals (right) attend Maryknoll School in Siuna, Nicaragua. Here you see seven good reasons why Maryknoll Sisters are in the gold-mining town of Siuna, Nicaragua. Humberto is the Sisters' best friend.

There's more to school than teaching, as Sister Virginia Therese (left) knows when Humberto brings her his new toy.

106

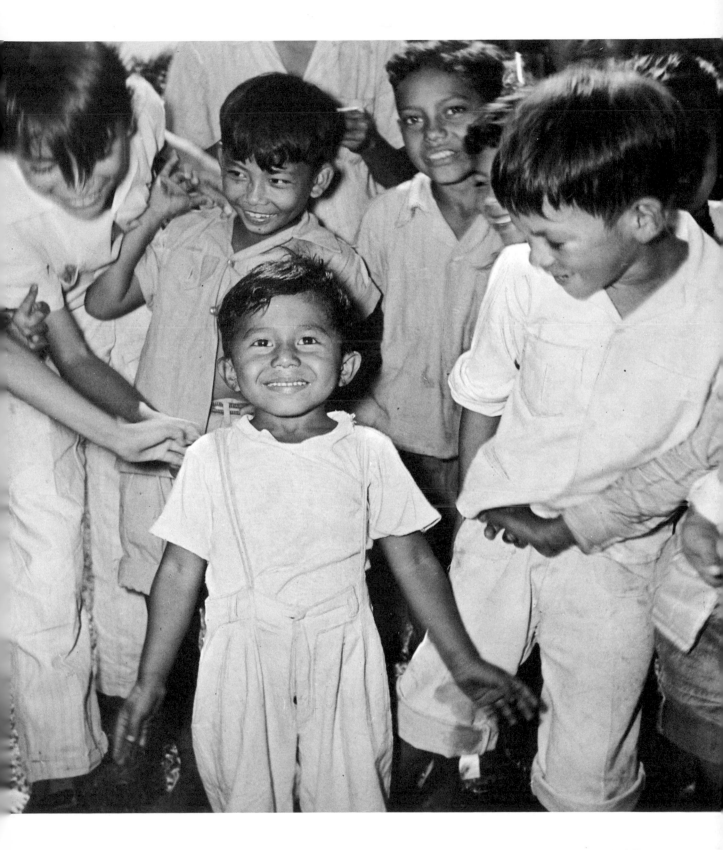

American troops clean out snipers from a bomb-blasted church on their way back into Manila at the end of the war.

LOS BANOS, P.I.

On April 11, 1944, the military police came to Assumption College in Manila where the Maryknoll Sisters were interned, and asked for Sister Trinita, the Regional Superior. After lengthy questioning, they searched Sister's belongings, and finally took her away to Fort Santiago, without permitting the other Sisters to speak to her. It was known that torture was used at Santiago, and Sister subsequently testified for the United States Government that she underwent torture several times. Later in the month the police came to the convent again, and this time took Sister Brigida.

On July 7th two military police came, and told the Sisters that they would be taken to a prison camp on the following day. Somehow the news got out among friends in Manila, and they were waiting for the Sisters at the gate when four trucks drew up to take them away. The Filipinos pressed their own sorely needed money into the Sisters' hands and tried to give them food, but the soldiers would not permit this. However, for the most part the Japanese soldiers were courteous and helpful. They lowered the truck's canvas sides for the ride through Manila so that the people would not see who their latest captives were. With five hundred other missioners, priests, Brothers, Sisters, Scholastics, Protestant ministers and their families, they went by truck to the train, and by train to Los Banos Camp, forty-two miles southeast of Manila.

Los Banos Camp already housed 1,100 internees. The missioners were assigned to a section with fourteen buildings—each one story high, with a wooden frame with woven bamboo sides and palm roofs. In a little while the whole section became known as Vatican Hill.

At first the menus were not too bad: breakfast—corn-rice mush, thin coconut milk, with coffee twice a week; dinner—rice and vegetable stew; supper—the same as dinner, with some-times a little carabao meat and a banana.

The Sisters entered into the camp organization, taking their places in the sewing squads, cleaning squads, KP squads, and so on. The Sister-nurses began to work in the general hospital, which was in charge of interned doctors. Two Assumption Sisters, one seventy-eight and the other sixty-nine, who had been kept two weeks in Iloilo, were brought into the camp. The Maryknoll Sisters took them in with great joy at being able to return in some small way the years of loving kindness showered on them by Mother Rose and her Community in Manila.

One of the barracks was converted into a chapel. On St. Dominic's Day the Dominican Fathers celebrated and the Maryknoll Sisters of St. Dominic sang the High Mass. They enjoyed two culinary specialties that day—coffee for breakfast and beans for dinner. "It takes a war," Sister Colman wrote from the camp, "to bring out the gustatorial value of the bean. It ranks near the top in our hierarchy of delicacies."

On August 22nd, they heard that Sister Brigida was out of Santiago and in the Philippines General Hospital. Excerpts from Sister Colman's account of the internment follows.

"Christmas came and it was a holy and blessed one. Two children and a young man were baptized the evening before. A Canadian Holy Cross Brother modeled a crib scene, and set it up with beautiful lighting effects. The Jesuit Scholastics woke us up with carols. The rustic barracks chapel was a perfect setting for Christmas Eve and we felt very close to the Holy Family and their Bethlehem cave.

"New Year's Day, 1945! At 7 A.M., returning from night duty in the Camp hospital, Sister Isabel passed Barracks 15, the Camp office. A weak voice called, 'Sister Isabel!' She turned, and could hardly believe her eyes that the emaciated figure at the desk was Sister Trinita. Japanese officials were filling out papers admitting her to the Camp. The Sisters had believed reports that Sister Trinita had been killed and seen lying dead on the street in Manila.

"Sister Isabel hastened to chapel and called Sister de Chantal out of Mass. Both hurried to Barracks 15 where they found Sister Trinita weak, but radiant. She had been brought in by troop train during the night. She was hurried home, bathed and tucked into bed—her first comfort in nine months. Sister had lost eighty pounds. She insisted on seeing all the Sisters and talked to them with great joy. Nothing could have rejoiced the Sisters more than this New Year's Gift.

"Tension began to mount in earnest. Food supplies were short and growing shorter. Planes came over daily and strafed the garrison. We were told to stay in our barracks except for roll call. Then the air raids began in earnest. Never could we have believed that we would so much enjoy the devastating sound of a bomb blast.

"Some of the civilians began to try to break out. Some were caught and executed, others made it.

"On February 1, the rations were cut again. Two weeks' supply was to last three weeks. We began a Novena to Our Lady of Lourdes for relief. More and more people died of starvation; a few more escaped. The food situation was desperate and Bishop Jurgens went to speak to Mr. Ito, the interpreter who had brought Sister Trinita and who had been most kind. A week later Episcopal Bishop Binstead also approached Mr. Ito. The answer came—no more rations. They gave out a supply of unhulled rice—but we could find no way to remove the hulls. Dr. Nance warned us not to eat it.

"The Japanese authorities stated definitely no more food would be issued and cryptically remarked that the next release would be quite different.

"On Friday, February 23rd, we attended our

Released from Los Banos prison camp on February 23, 1945, Maryknoll Sisters Maria del Rey (accepting candy) and Ancilla Marie enjoy kindness and candy from their welcome rescuers. They wore their "best clothes" to be rescued in.

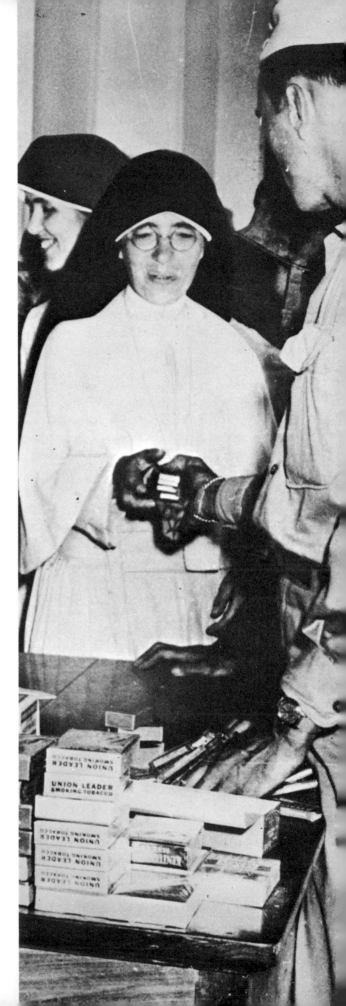

Community Mass in the dark as usual. The roll call gong sounded at seven and at the same time we heard planes. One of the Fathers near a window, breathed: 'Parachutes.'

"There was a dash for the windows and doors. Down our paratroopers came glistening like angel wings in the early morning light. Almost immediately we heard shots, and the battle for the camp was on. The Japanese tried to run back towards the hills but the Americans—giants, in uniforms we had never seen before, their faces grim, hard and determined—were after them and so were the Filipino guerrillas. Few, if any, of the Japanese escaped.

"About an hour later, one of the paratroopers came to the door of our barracks. 'It's over,' he said simply. 'It's been my dream to come and take you out.' We asked him where the army was. He explained that the area wasn't taken yet, but MacArthur had heard well authenticated reports that Tokyo had issued orders to execute all prisoners. He told us our forces were trying to hold back the Japanese for five hours while they got us out through the lines.

"We started moving fast. The soldiers helped in every way, courteous, smiling, friendly and helpful. A huge young paratrooper walked up to Sister Marion Cecilia and asked if she didn't remember him. It was her nephew—she had last seen him when he was five.

"The hospital patients went first, loaded on amphibian trucks, 30 to a truck. They rolled down to Lake Laguna two miles away and out onto the water. The barracks were set afire as we left. Japanese snipers and machine gunners fired constantly but the tank guns barked back. Two hours later we rolled onto another beach behind the American lines. The trucks turned around and headed back up the lake for the others.

"We were taken to Montinlupa, a prison, but it seemed like paradise. The soldiers offered every incoming internee chocolate bars and cigarettes. They served hot bean soup. They showed us our sleeping quarters in the prison cells, three-decker prison beds. Not luxurious but we had lights, water and abounding kindness everywhere. We were afraid to go to sleep lest we'd wake up and find it all a dream.

"We opened our eyes gingerly on Saturday morning to find we had not been dreaming! Two soldiers and not one paratrooper had been lost in the manoeuver. In commending his troops, General MacArthur issued a statement saying: 'God was certainly with us.' We had Mass and Communion in a beautiful chapel, and had much to give thanks for.

"They fed us in small portions lest the change from starvation be disastrous. The paratroopers were quartered here temporarily. Daily they drove out to combat amid the cheers of the internees. The fighting around was heavy and hundreds of refugees of every nationality were brought into the camp and cared for. Surely God will bless America for her wonderful generosity."

As the fighting moved away, things relaxed somewhat. Friends came out to Montinlupa to visit. Some of the Sisters returned to Manila. Shortly after Easter Sister Una and Sister Carmencita came from Baguio Mountain Province with news of the disappearance of Sister Hyacinth.

The three Sisters in Baguio, Filipina Sister Carmencita, Sister Una, who had an Irish passport, and Sister Hyacinth, who was seriously ill, had to turn over their convent to the Japanese on Christmas, 1944, and moved in with the Adoration Sisters. As the bombing became more severe, they moved into the mountains, living thereafter in a little compound of nipa huts. Throughout this time they were cared for by Gregorio Espiritu who had come to work for them one morning in 1930. In March, 1945, a trench he had dug in the hillside saved them in a bombing raid that killed seven Adoration Sisters. After that, the Maryknollers lived in a cave.

In April, 1945, the Igorot guerrillas urged them to move out through the Japanese lines because the Americans were planning to carpet-bomb Baguio. They and hundreds of others who had taken refuge in the hills gathered at an Evacuation Center very early Easter Monday morning, and started out through the mountains for Tubao, an American camp, with the Igorots acting as guides. They walked for four days.

Wednesday, between two resting places, Sister Hyacinth was lost. She had told Sisters Una and Carmencita that she would come more slowly with two Sisters of another Community and Gregorio. At the next resting place they waited for her, but she did not come. Finally Gregorio, who was carrying their food, arrived, and was surprised that Sister Hyacinth and her companions were not ahead of him. He went back immediately to the last resting place and on the way met the other two Sisters, who told him Sister had left them earlier hoping to catch up with Sisters Una and Carmencita. Meanwhile the caravan had moved on, and the Maryknoll Sisters were alone on the hilltop, when a guide found them. They explained their trouble and their desire to stay, but he urged them to get away quickly, for the area was very dangerous. Just then, as darkness began to fall, Gregorio got back, and the guide insisted for the safety of all that he and the Sisters move out of the area. Even so, it meant another night in the open, and they reached Tubao on Friday morning. Six runners were sent out at once to search for Sister Hyacinth, but no trace of her was ever found.

About half the Sisters were recalled to Maryknoll. On April 10, 1945, they boarded the SS *Eberle*. The ship was crowded, and they were instructed to stay below and wear their life jackets at all times. On May 2nd, they were reunited with their Maryknoll Sisters on the West Coast, and on May 9th were home at last at Maryknoll, New York.

In other parts of China there were great want and famine after the war. A starving boy still manages a cheerful smile for Sister-Doctor Antonia Maria at the clinic in Kweilin, 1949.

Sister Dominic Marie was one of the Maryknoll Sisters who went to Toishan, Kongmoon, in 1948 to staff a hospital. When the Communists took over China, the Sisters were ousted.

HONG KONG

On August 15, 1945 the Armistice came just when the Sisters thought they would all have to get out of China. The return to Hong Kong was a great deal more cheerful, but nearly as hazardous as the exodus.

The Sisters from Macao got back first, but found the school still being used as a Japanese military hospital. The three at the edge of India were given a ride in a doorless army cargo plane to Canton, from whence they traveled to Hong Kong by train, courtesy of Chinese General Ho Si Lai. Sister Paul couldn't get back from Kunming because of passport difficulties, until the RAF gave her and Sister Cecilia Marie a "lift" to Hong Kong. Sister immediately began negotiating for the return of the school building. Eventually they were allowed into one section, while the remainder housed six hundred Japanese who were still there when school reopened. The Sisters moved in on December 18th in a truck manned by Japanese war prisoners. On Christmas Eve the first Mass offered in the Convent for nearly three years was celebrated. School began on January 8th, in the building still shared by the prisoners.

MANCHURIA

With the end of the war the Sisters all over the world looked forward to returning to their beloved missions, but Manchuria was to remain closed. The Russians declared war on Japan seven days before the Armistice, and for their "war effort" were able to take over all of Manchuria and the Kurile Islands at the top of northern Japan.

The Sisters at the Russian Academy at Dairen were the first to taste Communist domination. While the Japanese authorities were still in control the enrollment had reached seventy, and the authorities had offered the five Maryknollers a wing of the Girls' High School.

However, the Russian takeover was in progress, and the Sisters, three Japanese, one Korean, and one German, all now enemy aliens, lived in well-founded fear of these soldiers.

Bishop Lane got to Dairen on December 23, 1945, and his presence was a great blessing. He had with him four Sisters of the local Fushun Community who were to work in Dairen, and he arranged for a resident Chinese priest to care for both the Chinese and the Japanese parishes. The Sisters struggled on, with the presence of the Communists a growing menace through 1945 and 1946. Other Maryknollers returned to Fushun for a few months but were unable to get in contact with their Sisters at Dairen.

CHINA

Throughout China the Sisters returned to their missions as quickly as they could. They got back to Pingnam on September 6, 1945, and reorganized the novitiate. This Community now had eight professed, two novices, one postulant, and thirteen aspirants. Later the novitiate was moved to Wuchow so that the aspirants could attend Girls' High School there. The Maryknoll Sisters also began again their catechetical work in this "City of No Conversions."

By 1947 they had opened a new mission at Sz Wong, four hours' walk from Pingnam.

When the Sisters got back to Kweilin at the end of 1945, they found their convent had been demolished. They began to rebuild both the Maryknoll Sisters' Convent and the novitiate for the Chinese Sisters. The lot of the people in this area was bitterly hard. There had been no crops for two years, and there was starvation everywhere. Money was useless, and barter was the only means of trade. However, the spiritual growth began again, and flourished.

Kaying had not been affected severely by the war, and the Sisters' missions had continued there. Under the direction of Bishop Ford, whose use of authority was such that it made hearts expand with confidence rather than contract with apprehension, the direct apostolate burgeoned.

The training given the national Sisters, here (left) working in the garden, was similar in all mission countries to that given Maryknoll's own Sisters, with emphasis on the wholeness in which holiness is based.

The Sisters of the Immaculate Heart (right) also received professional training in nursing, teaching, and catechizing to help them in their work for souls in their native land.

Three Sisters of the Immaculate Heart (left), trained for the religious life by the Maryknoll Sisters as one of their major mission works, pronounce their vows at Kongmoon in 1947.

The aged also suffered want as a result of the war, and Sister Rita Marie (right) sought them out when village visiting.

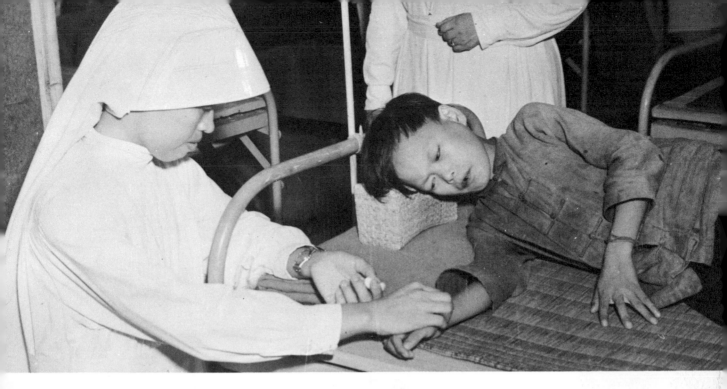

MARYKNOLL

Meanwhile at the Motherhouse in 1946 the fourth General Chapter—delayed three years because of the war—was called. Mother Mary Joseph retired with the title of Mother Foundress, and Mother Mary Columba was elected Mother General.

The following year a second Maryknoll novitiate was established in the United States at Valley Park, Missouri.

Around the world the missions had grown. In Hong Kong and in the interior of China they were flourishing: a new house was opened in Kaying and a hospital in Toishan. As yet, all seemed relatively peaceful in South China. A new school was opened in Hawaii and one in Cochabamba, Bolivia.

Air view of Maryknoll in the late 1930's. The seminary, at the lower left, was not yet completed. Rosary House, just behind the seminary tower, was—and still is—the Brothers' headquarters. Most of the small buildings in the center were later torn down to make way for the Publications Building built later. Pinesbridge Road cuts between the seminary and the new Motherhouse, upper right. The Cloister is beyond.

In 1939 Archbishop Spellman (now Cardinal) paid his first visit to Maryknoll as Archbishop of New York. Sister Mark, Motherhouse Superior, and Sister Eunice, General Councilor, see him to the door.

Archbishop Mitty of San Francisco presided at a Departure Ceremony for Sisters sailing from the West Coast in 1939. Sister Margaret Theresa kisses the ring.

(Left) *Signing the vow forms after the ceremony of profession in 1939. It was customary to sign them kneeling. Bishop James E. Walsh, then Superior General of the Maryknoll Fathers, also signs the legal form. He is now in a Communist prison in Shanghai.*

Reception of the habit (right). *The postulants are dressed in the Maryknoll habit but without a veil for the ceremony. They will receive the white veil that indicates they are now novices in the Order.*

Still crowded! The Motherhouse chapel (left), *built to accommodate two hundred Sisters, cannot hold the novices.*

(Right) *Taming the rugged terrain involves work. The lovely grounds at Maryknoll are, to a great extent, the work of the Sisters.*

Maryknoll Sisters on the go!

(Right) *Departure Ceremony held in the cloister court of the Motherhouse in 1946. Some sixty Sisters left for the missions of the world that year.*

(Left) *Novices walk through the woods at Maryknoll.*

(Right) *The grotto at Maryknoll. A favorite place for visitors, it was constructed by Ryozo Kado, Japanese rock artist, during World War II.*

(Left) *Broomstick, tin can, and snow—the makings of a perfect gentleman!*

(Right) *Winter or summer, someone is always saying the stations out of doors at Maryknoll.*

(Left) *Keeping the house running takes many hands to make light work. This is the switchboard operator* (above) *and a spinach-cleaning squad* (below).

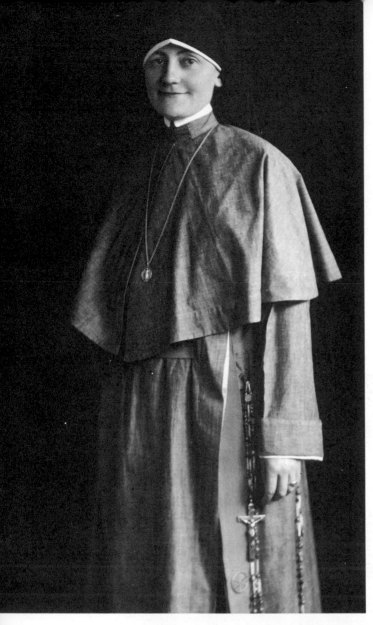

At the Chapter of 1946, Mother Mary Joseph retired, and Mother Mary Columba was elected Mother General. (Left) Mother Columba in 1927 when she went to Manila to direct the Maryknoll Sisters in the Philippines.

(Below) *Mother with her mother and sister just before she left for the Philippines.*

As she was, when, as Mother Columba, she took over the reins of government of a world-wide missionary order in 1946.

With Mother Mary Joseph (left) Mother Columba examines the Decree that made us an order of Pontifical status in 1954.

Saying goodbye to a young Sister going to Hong Kong in 1955.

(Above) *Departures for distant missions are the climax of the life at Maryknoll. They are always gay, even though they involve parting with many dear Sisters.*

(Right) *Maryknoll Teachers' College trains the Sisters in many phases of art as well as in educational subjects.*

JAPAN

Sisters Eva and Hostia returned to Japan—to Tsu, which had suffered bombings, tidal waves, and earthquakes. The view presented no Oriental temples and quaint teahouses—nothing but a flat, dreary expanse of rubble, dotted with shacks hastily built of salvage from bombing debris. Poverty was everywhere! That was February, 1947.

During the war years five Maryknoll Sisters, Sister Margaret, a Korean; Sisters Sabina, Rose Ann, and Talitha, Japanese; and Sister Marie Elise, German, were free in Dairen. The war years brought them less suffering than did the postwar period, when Russian soldiers took brutal possession.

On March 15th at 7:00 A.M., Sisters Rose Ann and Talitha were taken to a school building in Dairen to await repatriation. Here they were placed with thousands of others and told to wait. The next morning, at one o'clock, their examinations began. In their quarters there was not even room to stretch. Two meals of half-cooked rice and frozen potatoes boiled with fish bones were served each day. Many became sick.

The repatriation freighter, with three thousand people aboard, left Dairen on March 21st. There was no room to lie down. One old lady died on board, and a young lad succumbed shortly after they reached Japan. His sister had been converted by Sister Talitha, and she in turn baptized her brother.

The Sisters reached Kyoto on March 31st, where Father Felsecker took them in charge and Father Steinbach found a pair of new shoes for each of them. On the following Tuesday they drove out in the Fathers' jeep to Tsu and were reunited with their Maryknoll Sisters Eva and Hostia. "If only our other three in Dairen could be here!" they repeated over and over.

By May the Sisters opened a convent in Kyoto—the ancient capital city, 320 miles west of Tokyo, with a population of 1,200,000. This city of temples and beautiful gardens had been spared bombing both because of its cultural status and because no war materials were made there.

However, the city did not escape the prevalent poverty. Eggs were twenty cents each, and a small coverlet cost eight dollars. The main department stores had seven stories piled high with old clothes and family treasures sold to the store by the hungry.

The poor were in rags, and the money of the wealthy was frozen so they could not touch it. Food was rationed—each person was given only enough rice to cover five or six days a month; for the rest they had to tax their ingenuity to find sufficient food. Every square inch of land was cultivated to produce a few carrots, some cabbages, and the like.

Foreigners on entering Japan were required to bring a half-ton of food with them. That was the important question asked by the American Military when the Sisters arrived—Did you bring food? Americans were not to be a drain on the already terribly strained economy of the country.

The Sisters were shocked at the change, but profoundly grateful for the chance to return the good that had been done them by the Japanese before the war. In prewar days, when things had been difficult for foreigners in Japan, Manchuria, and Korea, the Sisters had many good, faithful friends among the Japanese who saw to their needs. Visiting the sick, alleviating pain and sorrow where possible, providing food, straightening out difficulties, teaching catechism in the convent and in homes took up the all too short hours of the day. The convent walls bulged on afternoons when the children flocked in to hear about God and to learn a little bit of English. Those were busy, busy days, with the happiness that goes with the joy of doing good.

In September, 1947, they welcomed Sisters Sabina and Margaret from Dairen. They had had a difficult voyage and at Shanghai had had to hide from the Russians in order not to be put back on the ship that had brought them from

The Sisters returned to Japan after the war and reopened their missions in the Kyoto area. Sister Hostia with a kindergarten class at Kyoto in 1948.

(Above) *Picnic day in Japan, and Sister Eva enjoys watching the boys wield their chopsticks with deft enthusiasm. The Sisters combined catechism classes with outings for the younger set of the parishioners.*

(Left) *The Catholic Church at one of the Kyoto missions was strictly Japanese in architecture and landscaping. Typically, the parishioners congregate outside after Mass on Sunday.*

129

Dairen. Sister Marie Elise was also released, but proceeded to the Philippines to visit her family there.

In 1948 another convent was opened at Nara, and the Kyoto convent became the center house with Sister Veronica Marie as Regional Superior and Sister Gloria in charge of Mission Arts.

Two more Maryknollers, Sisters Paul Miki and Jean, arrived from the States to begin language study.

They brought news to two new mission areas: one in the South Pacific Islands and the other in Africa.

TRUST TERRITORY

The South Pacific mission was on Koror, the chief island in the Palau group. At that time there were about nine hundred inhabitants on the island. Today there are two thousand. About a third of the people are Catholics, the rest Protestant or still pagan.

The Palauans raise their own food staples and get fish from the sea. They have an upper- and lower-caste system that limits the professions to which some of their people may belong. There are two levels of schools—elementary, grades one to six; and intermediate, grades seven to nine. After this, local girls may go on for nurses' training on Koror.

The Sisters—three of them—started a grade school in 1948 with the help of two Palauan girls who have since entered the Mercedarian Novitiate. By February, 1950, the ingenuity of the Jesuit Fathers had provided Mindzenty School, a nice two-story quonset hut, partitioned into six classrooms, with space on the second floor for boarders from the other islands. They had 150 students.

PHILIPPINES

This new mission was counted part of the Philippine region. The Sisters, in the midst of the rubble of war, had reestablished their college in

"Hi ya, Sister!" Sister Mary Karen gets a big greeting from a small Yapese. The Sisters have schools on four South Pacific Islands—Yap, Koror, Likiep, and Majuro.

Manila by July, 1945, and reopened the schools in Baguio, Malabon, and Lucena. St. Paul's Hospital had been demolished. However, they took over the operation of a hundred-bed hospital run for the workers of a sugar plantation in Manapla. Some of the graduate nurses of the hospital had been on the staff of this hospital before the war, and their capability and training had recommended Maryknoll to the plantation owners.

In addition to running the hospital the Sisters trained some of the older girls who worked with them to become catechists for their own barrios. The classes were held on the hospital lawn, and at first only about thirty children came. But the idea spread, and today over four hundred children, in many small groups, crowd about their young teachers every Sunday to hear the good word of God. The people—fun-loving, lighthearted Visayans—have been given a Catholic atmosphere in which to live, and have responded with a sincere interest in their Faith.

AFRICA

The other new mission land aroused tremendous excitement in the Community. Africa—now so much in the news and thought of in the world—was then an almost unconsidered continent among Americans, even among those who had been torn unwillingly from their homes and carried off to the Western Hemisphere. America hardly knew this ancestor of hers to whom she owed her spirit of heroic patience and rebounding joy; as she owed industry and steadfastness to her children from northern Europe, and her élan and imagination to her Latin background.

The Maryknoll Sisters were headed for Tanganyika, on the east coast of Africa, then a British Trust Territory under the United Nations. Sisters Stanislaus, Margaret Rose, Joan Michel, and Catharine Maureen arrived on December 27, 1948, in Kowak, near Lake Victoria in the northeast corner of Tanganyika. Fifteen years before, the White Fathers had opened this mission, and subsequently turned it over to the Maryknoll Fathers. The Sisters came to educate the girls for their Christian vocations in marriage, the religious life, or the professions; to improve health by instruction and medical care. Two of the Sisters were teachers, one a nurse and one a catechist.

They studied Swahili, the most general of the many languages used in Tanganyika. Later they would also have to learn the dialect local to the area in which they worked—and often several dialects when there were more than one tribe in the area.

They began three works in Kowak: the mission school, the native novitiate, and the dispensary.

Beginning with slates, the Sisters taught the basic rudiments. Sister Margaret Rose starts two small ones off on the Path of Learning in Kowak, near Lake Victoria.

Just a happy parish group chatting with Sister Marie William after Sunday Mass.

First departure for Africa, 1948. The Sisters knelt at Idlewild Airport, N.Y., to receive a multiple blessing from priests and then mounted the steps. Left to right (below), Sister M. Stanislaus, Sister Margaret Rose, Sister Catharine Maureen and Sister Joan Michel.

The primary school aimed at providing a basic education for the local girls, stressing health and homemaking.

The school was the only girls' school in an area about half as big as Massachusetts. According to custom, the Sisters added a grade each year. They followed the Syllabus of Instruction for African Schools in Tanganyika, which included a daily period for religion and several hours for gardening. All the textbooks were in Swahili. By August, 1950, they had sixty-two pupils, some of them coming from thirty miles away.

On the whole the Africans of these parts considered education rather harmful for a girl, but they wanted to have their sons educated. This meant the daughters herded the cattle, so that it was doubly hard to persuade parents to let their girls come to school.

The first- and second-graders were somewhat older than usual, since this was their first chance to get an education. Second-graders ranged from ten to fourteen, the oldest girls being already eligible for marriage, and for some the dowry of cows that is the marriage contract of the area had already been paid. In the short time these girls remained in school the Sisters strove to give them the basics of the three R's and to open their hearts to new ideas and principles.

The work to improve health was only beginning. The people suffer from dysentery, hookworm, and bilharzia because of complete lack of sanitation, contaminated water supply, and ignorance of the causes of infection and contagion. Malnutrition is prevalent because of the heavy, starchy diet. The government has planted papaya and other fruit trees that grow rapidly, but they are unfamiliar to the Africans, who have not yet learned how to cultivate them. The gardening periods were given to helping these trees grow, and the basic needs of a balanced diet became part of the lessons taught.

The second work at Kowak was the novitiate for Sisters for the Musoma Prefecture. This Sisterhood will have as its work teaching and medical apostolate. The problem of local teachers is pressing in Tanganyika, where most girls marry so early that even trained teachers cannot be counted on to continue in their profession for more than a very few years.

The novitiate was a one-room native house of mud with a grass roof, with another hut nearby used as the kitchen. Eleven girls began their training, with the youngest (under fourteen) attending the mission school, while the older ones received private instruction in reading, writing, arithmetic, and geography. All eleven were instructed in religion, Christian Ethics, general deportment, and health.

The aspirants could bring nothing with them except the dresses they were wearing, since by entering this life they are causing their families, most of them still pagan, to sacrifice twenty or more cows, which would have been given as a dowry.

The Kowak Mission Dispensary provided medical care for patients who did not require hospitalization, the nearest hospital being thirty miles away. In the first ten months, eight thousand patients were treated. This number does not include home visits made in serious emergencies.

Drugs were purchased at a discount in Kenya, and bandages came from the States, mostly as gifts, as did the instruments, sphygmometer, stethoscope, and microscope. One gift defrayed the cost of an examination table, and another made possible the purchase of a native bed for deliveries, which previously were done on a mat on the floor.

The infant mortality rate was 70 percent; there was no public or private sanitation. Leprosy was considered hereditary, and the victims were accepted by family and community, who naturally failed in the simple precautions that could prevent its spread. It was estimated that thirty of every thousand Luos were afflicted.

Many women began to come in for deliveries in the hope of saving their babies. This was an opportunity for adult education in health and diet. A maternity hospital was badly needed.

The clinic line keeps Sister Agnes Jude busy. At first the Sisters wore helmets as protection from the equatorial sun.

First fruits of the work. Sister Margaret Rose and First Communicants at Kowak in 1949.

CEYLON

Another new area was opened to the Sisters when they received a request from the Ceylonese Government through Benedictine Bishop Bernard Regno of Kandy, Ceylon, to staff part of a six-hundred-bed civil hospital there.

The first group arrived on August 17, 1949, and opposition to them ran high in this center of Buddhist worship. That the Sisters were there in a purely professional capacity was made clear from the beginning. However, some opposition continued. The Kandyans themselves, however, proved loyal friends, and the sick poor showed their gratitude in many loving ways.

The government hospital is situated in Kandy, the old hill capital city, with a population of 800,000. The majority of the citizens are Sinhalese, next Tamils, some Burghers (Dutch or Portuguese), and some Eurasians. In the center of the city is the famous Buddhist Temple of the Tooth, whence flows the culture and religion of the people. It is a stronghold of Buddhism, and the yellow-robed monks can be seen in numbers in the town. They are most faithful in visiting the wards of the hospital on Sundays and Poya (full-moon) days, when they preach and chant. Attendants and patients alike show them the greatest reverence.

Of the patients, 70 percent were Buddhist, 15 percent Hindu, 8 percent Muslim, 3 percent Catholic, 3 percent Protestant. In addition to caring for these patients, the Sisters taught obstetrics, midwifery, and pediatrics. The teaching had to be done in Sinhalese, and the Maryknollers were glad that, despite advice to the contrary, they had proceeded with language study as is their custom.

Their apostolate was very indirect, being that of good example and the presence of Christ in the midst of His children.

The Sisters had never been able to get back to the missions in North Korea that had been given to the Communists as a reward for their seven-day war against Japan. One Maryknoll Sister alone remained in Korea: Sister Mary Agneta Chang, a Korean, had stayed throughout the war as novice mistress of the Korean Community of Our Lady of Perpetual Help in Pyeng Yang, which the Maryknoll Sisters had been training.

In December, 1949, three Sisters arrived in Pusan and opened a clinic. In June, 1950, Communists from North Korea poured into the South. The war was on, and the Sisters were evacuated to Japan.

No more news of Sister Agneta came out of Korea for many months. The evacuated Maryknollers asked and obtained the permission of General Douglas MacArthur to return to Pusan. Sisters Mercy, Rose of Lima, and Augusta flew back on March 19, 1951, They were the first civilian women permitted in the war area. Their clinic was desperately needed by thousands of refugees fleeing the Red horror in the North, and they quickly asked for and received additional Sisters from the Orient and the States. The ill and needy swarmed into Pusan, and at one point the Sisters were treating over two thousand patients daily in what has been called "the longest Charity Line in the world."

Among the refugees there were a few of the Sisters of Perpetual Help with the tragic story of Sister Agneta's living martyrdom and most probable death. She was harassed, questioned, and tormented by the Communists both for her Faith and for the sake of her brother John, later Premier of South Korea. At last the Sisters, by then in lay clothes, tried to hide her in out-of-the-way villages. She was, however, eventually betrayed and carried off by the Communists in an oxcart, on October 4, 1950. She was never heard of again. Rumors reported her killed and buried in a trench with other victims.

The Maryknoll Sisters' Clinic at Pusan, Korea, is an oasis of hope to thousands of refugees who streamed into South Korea when Communists took over the North. Sister Augusta and Sister Agnus Therese tend a boy in a cast for spinal tuberculosis.

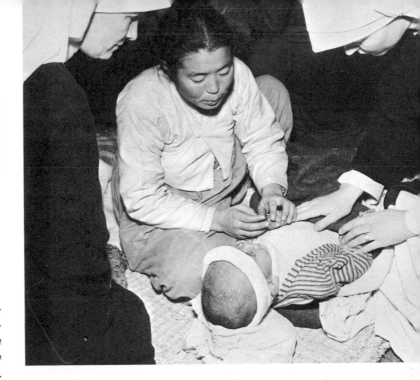

When the Korean War began in 1950, the Sisters were evacuated, but soon received permission from General Douglas MacArthur to return and reopen the badly needed clinic. Sister Edith Marie is surrounded by people who need help.

Maryknoll Sister-Doctor Agnus Therese and a Korean Sister return from sick-call duty in the hills outside Pusan. Warships of many nations crowd the harbor, and barbed wire surrounds an army installation.

Francis Cardinal Spellman (right) is serenaded by a young Korean during a Christmas visit to the Pusan Clinic. The anxious music teacher in the background is Sister Herman Joseph, a medical technician.

Outside the clinic (above) Sister Kathleen Marie checks the line to locate the most critically ill among hundreds of sick. For three years they cared for over two thousand patients daily.

General Maxwell Taylor (below) signing papers allocating materials for the Maryknoll Sisters Armed Forces Memorial Hospital in Pusan, in April, 1954. Captain Voyles and Sister Rose of Lima, a pharmacist, watch.

CHINA

By now the takeover in China was well under way. In Wuchow section the Communists took control on November 25, 1949, but for a year there was comparative calm.

On December 19, 1950, the Communists declared martial law. Communist troops entered the school and convent, and the soldiers searched the house, meanwhile planting a packet of opium in Sister Rosalia's room. There they "discovered" it. Sister Rosalia was arrested and imprisoned, as were Maryknoll Bishop Frederick Donaghy and Father Justin Kennedy. The remaining Sisters were held under house arrest until expelled. Sister Rosalia was released and expelled in May, 1951.

At Sz Wong in February, 1951, two Sisters were interned in the attic of the Mission. Sister Barbara Marie became very ill, but Sister Rose Bernadette could not persuade the Communists

to give her any medicine. They remained in their garret throughout the summer and into the winter. In November, 1951, with Sister Barbara Marie still ill, Sister Rose Bernadette was removed to Wuchow. All her Maryknoll Sisters had gone, and the now eighteen Chinese Sisters were in lay clothes, scattered in small groups, trying to carry on their apostolate in secrecy. In the following month Sister Rose Bernadette was expelled. Sister Barbara Marie was finally expelled in January, 1952. She was the last Maryknoll Sister to leave Wuchow.

The story was repeated in Kweilin, Yeungkong, Loting, and Kaying. The Maryknoll Sisters were all expelled in March, 1951. They left behind fourteen professed Sisters in the Chinese Community, and 3,700 Catholics, not counting the hundreds of refugees who had been baptized during the war years.

Sisters Colombiere, Candida Maria, and Mon-

A Chinese Sister with a girl who wishes to join the Order. Trained by Maryknoll Sisters, the Chinese Sisterhoods have largely become autonomous, and in lay clothes continue good work behind the bamboo curtain.

The Maryknoll Sisters of Kaying, China, taken after the 1948 retreat with the retreat master Jesuit Father Patrick Joy and their Bishop Francis X. Ford. Within five years the bishop was dead in a Communist jail and the Sisters were expelled from the mainland.

ica Marie were arrested and imprisoned in Loting, and eventually expelled from China. The Yeungkong missioners were confined briefly and then given exit permits.

Kaying, which had been nearly untouched by the war, suffered most severely. In the December, 1950, Bulletin for the Kaying Diocese, Bishop Ford wrote: "The restrictions [against public assembly] have been somewhat arbitrarily extended to several parishes in the prefecture, as regards catechumenates. The enforced 'Silent Night' repeating the very first Christmas, will still echo the angels' serenade in our hearts."

On December 3, 1950, the first four Maryknollers were arrested—Father Dennis, Father Bogaard, Sister Marie Marcelline, and Sister Paul Therese in Laofuheo. The soldiers had planted bullets among the Sisters' belongings. The Chinese Sister-Catechists of Our Lady, who had been in their care, were disbanded. The Maryknollers were held in prison for fifty days, released briefly so that they could suffer the experience of having their Catholic people fear to approach them, incarcerated again, and finally sentenced on St. Patrick's Day, 1951, to "leave China."

Bishop Ford sent directions to the Chinese

priests and Religious to discard their habits, disband, and get into their homes, continuing their work from these "catacombs."

On December 23, 1950, Bishop Ford and his entire staff were arrested. For seven months the five Kaying Sisters were confined to one basement room; Sister Joan Marie, who had been Bishop Ford's secretary, was placed in solitary confinement after months. The other four were expelled in July, 1951. Of six Sisters in one of the mission stations, five were expelled in October, 1951, after nearly a year's imprisonment. The remaining one, Sister Margaret Marie, a Chinese-American, continued to work in the area, together with Maryknoll Father Maynard Murphy, until they too were ousted in October, 1952.

At Hingning two Maryknoll Sisters were taken to the public trial of their pastor, Father Aloysius Au. The Sisters stood in the sun for six hours, while the priest was slandered and reviled, and the people were encouraged to throw dirt and stones at the Maryknollers. Father Au was given an extended jail sentence. The Sisters were expelled.

Sister Joan Marie remained in confinement. On occasions she caught a glimpse of Bishop Ford and saw that he was worn out, with black circles under his eyes. He was subjected to continual questioning. This went on until April 13, 1951.

After a staged demonstration against them in Kaying, Bishop Ford was bound, and he and Sister were taken to Canton. The Communists had planned demonstrations against them along the way. At Hingning, the first stop, they were taken off the bus and paraded in the streets. They were met with a wall of shouting, screaming Middle School students who had been worked up to a frenzy. The youngsters were armed with sticks, stones, and refuse. The Bishop walked slowly and deliberately through the lines, followed by Sister. Blows rained on them both. The students put sticks between the Bishop's legs, and when he fell they beat him badly.

Finally, in the general melee, the guards were also beaten, and ran, leaving the Bishop and Sister Joan Marie at the mercy of the frenzied students. However, they proceeded calmly, refused to run, and took the abuse without complaint.

The procedure was repeated at Laulung and Ho-yun. There heavier ropes were put on the Bishop. They had been soaked in water so that they would contract when they dried out. The abuse at Canton was the worst.

The two Maryknollers were finally brought to Canton prison and searched thoroughly. Sister was crowded with seventeen other women into a small room, big enough for eight people.

Living conditions in the prison were very bad. Sister was assigned to a work squad carrying water. Each prisoner, however, was given only two cups of water a day. They had no towels, no soap, no toothbrushes, no washbasins. Sister had only her habit and one change of underwear. She slept on the stone floor with a summer quilt for covering. The Bishop was in the same predicament. In July, 1951, she caught a glimpse of him, and he seemed well. The following December Bishop Ford sent her his old smoking jacket, a kimono, a heavy quilt, a pillow, and mosquito net. He had received these things from Kaying. Sister suspected that he had received only this bundle, and tried to return it to him, but the guard told her that if she did not take it it would be sent to the prison.

Though her work made it possible for Sister to move around a bit, she did not see the Bishop again until January, 1952. She was standing near a stairway that branched off into various corridors, when her bare foot slipped and she fell to her knees. As she began to rise she glanced through slits in the bamboo door before her and saw a prisoner being carried down the stairs, thrown over the shoulder of another prisoner like a sack of potatoes. It was Bishop Ford, evidently being brought down from the roof where he may have been taken for some air and sun. Just then the prisoner stood him up and said,

"Come on. Walk." The Bishop stood with his legs apart, arms outstretched, trying to keep his balance. He strained to move his feet, but finally said, "I can't walk." The other prisoner came over and pulled him along. The Bishop's hair was white, as was his long, bushy beard. He was plainly very weak.

Sister saw him again two days later, but now walking slowly, leaning on a stick and on another prisoner's arm. Later in the month she saw him again being carried upstairs by a prisoner, and once more in early February. She never saw him again. She felt that he could hardly survive on the insufficient food, sleeping on a stone floor, and completely lacking care.

Her own brainwashing and interrogation continued. Of all these awful hours, Sister recalled later the following incident. She writes: "At the time I did not appreciate the humorous aspect of it, for I was concerned only with answering the question. If we really tried to confuse them, I don't think we could have done much better!

"The interrogation group around the table said: 'We wish you to tell us exactly the details of your joining the imperialistic spy organization, the Catholic Church: When, where, and the name of the person who introduced you. His age, address, and education.'

"I answered: 'But it is not a spy organization . . .'

"They interrupted: 'Don't talk so much. Answer the question honestly and frankly, and don't talk about things you are not asked about. Now, begin; where did you join the organization?'

"I said: 'In New York.'

" 'Good. When did you join the organization?'

" 'I was very young.'

" 'How young?'

" 'Two weeks old. I was born a Catholic.'

"This startled them, and the secretary looked up, but the second interrogator understood and suavely remarked: 'Oh, you were born a Catholic? Is your family Catholic?' (The implication was my entire family were members of a spy ring.)

" 'Yes,' I replied; 'my family are Catholic.'

"The head interrogator relaxed as the possibility of this confession became clear to him. He smiled and nodded. Then, leaning across the table toward me, he said slowly and deliberately: 'When did your family join up, who is responsible, who introduced them? Be frank and honest. You will not get away with it if you are not open with us.'

"I said: 'I don't know, it was long ago. It's impossible to say.'

"They shouted at me: 'Dishonest talk! Answer the question.'

"So I answered truthfully: 'My family joined the Church through the influence of a man named Patrick.'

"That pleased them. 'When did this happen?'

" 'A long time ago, I cannot say when.'

" 'You tell us when,' they insisted.

"I tried to recall dates, but couldn't: 'I can't remember. About seven hundred years ago.'

"I was close to tears, but I remember the effect was somewhat that of a pricked balloon. Their 'scoop' hadn't come off. The chief interrogator turned to the others and sighed in Mandarin: 'What's the use.'

"He called the guard to take me away.

"A few incidents like this gave me the reputation among the comrades of being clever—but it was just simplicity. The thing to remember is that these men are deadly serious and fully believe the propaganda against the Church."

Sister became very ill and was removed to a hospital for a time, but returned to prison on July 28th.

The summer wore on, and in preparation for the Assumption, on August 15th, Sister began nine days of special prayers to Our Blessed Mother for news of the Bishop. On the 16th she was called to the head office and told that Bishop Ford had died. Although she had seen his pitiful condition, this news came as a dreadful shock to her. She later recounted it herself:

" 'He died of old age and illness,' the officer went on. 'We gave him the very best care at the Central Hospital, the best hospital in Canton. He was there a very long time; his illness was slow.'

"Still I could say nothing.

" 'I have photographs here to prove what I say,' the man continued, and let me see the pictures. The first showed a large hospital room with French windows and curtains. A nurse stood by the bed; a doctor held the wrist of the patient. It all looked very posed. In the bed was, undoubtedly, Bishop Ford. His head was swathed in bandages. The little woolen skull cap he usually wore was on top of the bandage. He was clean shaven so that the emaciation was evident, his cheek bones high and his eyes sunken.

"He showed me other pictures of the Bishop either dying or already dead with glazed eyes and gaping mouth.

" 'Will you give me copies of these photographs?' I asked. He promised but I never got them. The officer brought forward another paper—a death certificate. Date of death: February 21, 1952. Cause: Illness and old age.

" 'He had the best care,' the officer repeated. 'The best hospital in Canton, doctors and nurses. But it was a long illness; they couldn't save him.'

"I remembered I had seen him in the prison early in February, and the date of death given was February 21. He was only 60 years old.

" 'Sign it,' the officer ordered, handing me a paper saying Bishop Ford had died in Central Hospital of illness and old age. It took forcing, but I signed it."

Her illness flared up again, her temperature rocketed to 105 degrees, and they sent her back to the hospital. There, suddenly, they gave her everything possible—vitamins, calcium, liver, eggs, milk—the whole range of build-me-ups. Later, Sister learned this was standard Communist procedure. Before a prisoner is released, they put a little meat on his bones so he won't look too bad, and his stories will not sound so true.

She asked to see Bishop Ford's grave, and on her way back to prison, on September 1st, they took her out to the suburbs to an old Chinese cemetery. There was one new grave, with a common marker on which in fresh red paint was written: *Fouc Ni Tet Mou*—the Bishop's name and the word "grave." No date.

The next morning the guard came and told her to pack up. She was brought to the officer in charge, who announced: "Much more evidence has been found against Bishop Ford. It will be made public on September 10th, and the reaction will be terrific. To save you from being torn apart when the people learn the true iniquity of Bishop Ford, we are deporting you."

Sister tried once more to get the pictures of Bishop Ford, but failed. They told her the film had been spoiled in the darkroom.

A male and a female officer brought her to the station, paid her fare because she had no money, and escorted her to the border. No one knew she was coming, and there was no one to meet her. At the Hong Kong exit from China, the Communists went through each person's bundles as he went out.

As the man glanced through Sister's meager bundle, he whispered to her: "Don't worry, Sister. You'll come back."

She walked uncertainly across the No Man's Land between the Red Hell and freedom, her mind completely preoccupied with the fact that she had no passport and that the British were very particular about a passport for people coming into Hong Kong. She cautiously approached the British soldier on border guard, and said, "I don't have a passport, but I'm a Maryknoll Sister and my Sisters in the Colony will identify me."

The soldier smiled lazily at her: "You don't need a passport, Sister. Your face is passport enough." He brought her to the British Police Inspector Mr. Robson, who bought her ticket for the train and notified the manager of the railroad, who in turn notified the Maryknoll Sisters in Hong Kong. Maryknoll Brother Francis met the train, and escorted Sister to Kowloon. That evening she was home with her Maryknoll Sisters.

Sister Joan Marie (Ryan) was kept in jail by the Communists for two years and four months and then banished from China. When she recovered her health she was reassigned to the China missions on Formosa, and this photograph was taken just before she left in 1959.

Good Measure, Pressed Down
/ 1950 to 1962

BY 1952 COMMUNIST HATRED had closed thirty-four Maryknoll mission convents in the Orient. By 1962 American generosity had opened seventy-eight new missions around the world.

One morning in the fall of 1961 two young African women stood at the top of the staircase in New York City's Grand Central Terminal and watched two Maryknoll Sisters hurry across the main concourse to catch a train for Ossining.

"Good morning, Sisters," the girls called out, and ran down the stairs. The Sisters stopped, and smiled with delight and surprise.

"We thought you were in Indiana," they told the girls.

"Not yet. One more weekend in New York, and then we go."

"What have you been doing, buying out the city?"

"Not exactly, Sister, just a few things. Everything is wonderful, though, isn't it?"

The Sisters laughed. "Do you believe the price tags yet," one of them asked, "or are you still bargaining?"

The girls smiled ruefully. "Not any more, Sister. But there's not much fun in shopping if you can't bargain."

They talked until the Sisters' train was ready to go. "God bless you," the Maryknollers said. "Do your best at college."

"We will, Sisters. Thank you."

The Maryknollers smiled as they hurried to catch their train. Those two girls were part of a big success story from the Sisters' point of view. They were two of five African women, graduates of the Sisters' high school in Morogoro, Tanganyika, who had won scholarships to continue their education in the United States. Of the fifteen girls in that first graduating class, every one had passed the difficult and lengthy Cambridge Overseas Examination. A decade earlier, when they first came to Tanganyika, the Maryknoll Sisters had at Kowak one catechumenate, one clinic, two grades of elementary school, and a few aspirants to an African Community.

The Sisters opened Marian College in Morogoro in 1957, and Rosary College in Mwanza in 1961. There are only two other complete high schools for girls in all Tanganyika. In this nation of 9,000,000 there are in 1962 fewer than ten Tanganyikan women with college degrees. In December, 1958, Sister Margaret Rose, one of Maryknoll's pioneer four to Africa, and at that time principal of the Monogoro high school, wrote: "The future holds great promise both for our high school and for its alumnae. The task of the moment is to find proper work for them in vital fields. Education, medicine, communications, the press; all could use responsible young women, but there is little or no precedent to guide the girls.

"For those who can continue their studies, we dream of scholarships to colleges abroad until the day dawns when East Africa has its own Catholic University.

"Ultimately the future for the girls is to be the wives of the leaders of tomorrow's Tanganyika, and the mothers of Tanganyika's future children. That 'tomorrow' is nearer than we dare to dream. We pray that their education at Marian College will prepare them for the responsibility that will be theirs whatever they choose to do with their lives."

Now Tanganyika has stepped across the threshold to freedom and independence, and her need of professional men and women to guide her wisely has become acute. Even before Independence Day, December 9, 1961, Mary Kasindi, one of the teachers at Marian College, was a member of the National Assembly.

At the grass-root levels the Sisters' work of catechetics, medical assistance, and education depends heavily on home visiting. Sister Joan Michel, superior of Shinyanga, and one of the first four, explains this work. "We feel that family visiting has a very definite and important place in the apostolate of the Church in Africa. Here, as in many of our mission fields, we labor among simple folk to whom the slightest courtesy or interest means a great deal. Many of our mission territories have felt the exploitation of

the 'Europeans,' as white people are generally called by the Africans. We missioners come as apparent members of this group, but through the Faith of our Christians we are accepted as something more. Even the pagan looking on recognizes that here is something different. Therefore it is up to us to prove that we have their interest at heart.

"Teaching and waiting for them to come to the mission is not enough. Here is where a visit can impress the African in a real and concrete way; showing them that we are interested in them, not merely as someone to fill the pews on Sunday, but in everything that goes to make up their lives. Meeting them in their own surroundings, talking with them in their own homes and fields has a great potentiality for good. It is not enough to teach the Commandments and instruct them in the Sacraments in their own tongue. The missioner must also know a little something about the grain and the maize they grow, and have some understanding of their struggles to make a livelihood. We cannot convince them that the Christian way of life is made up of prayer, work, and play, unless we meet them in all these activities, and show an interest and desire to know more and to identify ourselves with them as much as possible."

The Charity of Christ had urged the Sisters to bring the good news of Christ's love to Tanganyika, and with it they brought a torrent of other gifts: the opportunity to choose a religious life if God gave that vocation; the opportunity to obtain the finest quality education; the opportunity to receive hospital care, professional nursing care, to have well-baby clinics for their little ones, homemaking and hygiene classes for adults.

As the five Tanganyikan students began their college careers in the United States, the Maryknoll Sisters in their country had increased to more than forty, and included a doctor, a pharmacist, three midwives, more than a dozen nurses, a social service worker, and twoscore teachers. Their works had also expanded to in-

Sister-nurse, accompanied by a nurse's aide from the Riberalta hospital, brings modern medical care to an impoverished upriver family.

Music class (above) *at Santa Rosa School in Lima. Pupil enrollment in all Maryknoll's schools in Latin America has rocketed since the Sisters first began educational work there.*

In Nicaragua, Siuna schoolboys learn how to hold a censer as their first step toward becoming altar boys.

clude instruction of over 800 catechumens and nearly 600 newly baptized Catholics; one national Community with six professed, two novices, and 104 aspirants; two high schools and three elementary schools with over 900 students; a hospital and four clinics serving over 50,000 patients annually. A regular program of adult education had also been inaugurated.

Through the years Kowak had become but part of the exotic-sounding Tanganyikan missions: Kowak, Nyegina, Rosana, Shinyanga, Morogoro, Makoko, Mwanza, and Nassa.

"Come to our house, Sister!" Children from one of the Sisters' schools in Chile lead their teacher across a wobbly bridge on their way home. Home visiting is part of the work in all the Latin American missions.

LATIN AMERICA

On June 26, 1961, sixty-five teachers, both lay and religious, from various Congregations, met in Riberalta, Bolivia, for a six-day Teachers' Institute. For such a thing to happen in that isolated jungle town with its grass-grown streets was almost a miracle. In proposing such an Institute, Maryknoll Sister Bernard Mary explained: "I am inviting teachers from seven schools in the area to exchange ideas and help one another grow professionally in order to be better prepared to fulfill our role in the Church's teaching apostolate.

"The principal aim of the Institute is to give in-service training to our Catholic lay teachers, who, for the most part, have had no pre-service training. As Catholic teachers, they are 'co-workers in the cause of Christ' and it is our obligation to prepare them to carry out this responsibility.

"While we have the lay teacher particularly in mind, we feel that the Sisters, too, will be able to profit much from listening, discussing and presenting problems in an informal gathering. Since we all work under similar conditions, we, no doubt, have like problems and should find help in discussing them with others."

At the Institute, papers were presented on: Catholic Philosophy of Education; Professional Ethics; Human Relations in the Classroom; Teaching Techniques and Disciplines; Religion Methods; Reading Methods; Hygiene; and Purity and the Emotional Development of the Latin Girl. After each paper there was a period for general discussion. One special session was held for teachers and directors at each of the various grade levels.

As a practical contribution to the Institute, the Maryknoll Sisters had mimeographed all the lessons for the Sixth Grade, so that they could be passed out to the children to be kept in looseleaf folders as they were ready to study them. This is part of the Sisters' effort to eliminate the blackboard-to-notebook copying routine that eats up all the teaching time. During

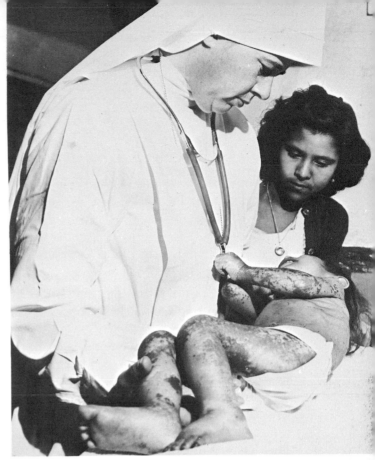

The Madre-Doctora, Sister Rose Cordis of Jamaica Plain, Massachusetts, was assigned to Guatemala as a result of the thumbprint petition of the Indians of Jacaltenango. Sister reaches the various Maryknoll mountain clinics by horseback.

An Aymara Indian mother (right), *in the typical high white hat and colorful shawl, and her baby, who is sporting a peaked wool cap. The Sisters conduct schools in the Peruvian Andes for the Indian children.*

the Institute itself, together with other teachers, they planned lessons for the other grades, which they hope to mimeograph and present at the next Institute.

The Institute was a significant step in the growth and development of the Maryknoll Sisters' work in Latin America. When they first came, the Sisters found the people willing to have their children educated, even though, in their poverty, it ordinarily involved a sacrifice for them. When necessary the parents even agreed to pay tuition in order to pay the lay teachers' salaries.

It was generally the custom not to have boys and girls in the same school, but often this amounted to depriving the boys of an education. The Sisters took them in at the grade-school level, and the parents went against custom to send them.

The teaching method on their arrival consisted in a tedious copying of notes from the blackboard to a rough copybook, and then at home to a clean copybook. Few students completed primary school, much less secondary, although there were only six grades in primary. The Sisters, therefore, had to train alert students as teachers in their schools, by instituting training courses during the summer vacations and giving them in-service instructions in the classrooms. Elsa, one of these student-teachers in Galvarino, Chile, was able to complete her high-school education through money sent from the States by a group of American women for the specific purpose of training a student to become a teacher.

In Bolivia a grade school in Cobija opened in 1946 with 25 girls in first and second grades. Today there are 500 pupils. A rural school in Riberalta, with classes scheduled from 8:30 A.M. to 1:00 P.M. so that the children can help their parents in the fields, rocketed from 45 students in 1943 to over 1,000 today. The single major factor, the Sisters believe, is the personal interest they and their lay teachers have in each child. This has convinced the parents that the Maryknoll schools were in earnest about helping their children learn.

Adding to their work in Bolivia, Nicaragua, and Panama, the Maryknoll Sisters in 1950 went to Chile and Mexico. That year there were 50 Maryknoll Sisters in Latin America. A decade later there were 180 Sisters conducting: 31 schools, including 8 high schools and one college, with a total of 10,000 pupils; two hospitals and seven clinics caring for 156,000 patients a year; and two national novitiates. The Sisters had missions in seven towns in Chile, five in Peru, seven in Bolivia, five in Guatemala, two in Panama, one in Nicaragua. They had 173 lay teachers in their schools.

Medical work had been the first effort in Latin America, and it still has the flavor of a great adventure. Riberalta, that city of beginnings, was the site of the Sisters' first hospital. In addition to the usual variety of semitropical diseases—malaria, worms, malnutrition—the Sisters handled operations including emergencies caused by machete wounds and the mauling of wild animals. The ambulance was as often as not a hammock, a dugout canoe, or the Fathers' motor launch.

The mission work in Panama included buying and wrapping Christmas presents for every pa- *tient at the leprosarium at Palo Seco in the Canal Zone.*

Three Sister-doctors now work in Guatemala, Peru, and Bolivia; fourteen Sister-nurses are in school clinics or riding mountain trails in Guatemala and Nicaragua, and jungle rivers in Bolivia, Peru, and Chile to reach their patients.

In 1958 the Indians of Guatemala put in their bid for medical aid. Mother Mary Colman was completing a visitation of the missions in Latin America, where nearly every Bishop and priest had assured her that the needs of his people were the most urgent. The Indians of Guatemala were at the end of a long, long list. Mother promised them a Sister-nurse, but they knew they needed a doctor because their craggy mountain land makes it nearly impossible for them to reach a hospital when they need to most. They made their point. A group of men went through the town of Jacaltenango and its outlying villages and got their neighbors to put their X and their thumbprint on a document avowing that they needed a Sister-doctor. One of their greatest griefs was the appallingly high infant-mortality rate. An Indian guide told Mother that of his thirteen children only one had lived. The man entrusted with presenting the thumbprint document to Mother almost

didn't make it. He reached her in the town plaza just as she was about to begin the six-hour horseback trip out through the mountains. He apologized for delaying her. He was late because his wife had died in childbirth that morning.

There was no need to say more. In 1960 Sister-doctor Rose Cordis and four Sister-nurses were assigned to Guatemala. The Indians themselves built a hospital at Jacaltenango, and in addition the Sisters opened three clinics in mountain villages.

The emphasis in these countries, where almost all are baptized Catholics, is placed on an active participation in the Mass and reception of the Sacraments, both long neglected for lack of priests and owing to a false attitude of piety. The Sisters' aim is always to train catechists from among the local people, who in turn instruct their neighbors in the Faith.

During school vacations the Sisters accompany the priests on mission trips to remote areas. Horses, jeeps, dugouts, motorboats are all used to reach out-of-the-way mountain pueblos or river settlements. During their stay at these villages, the Sisters live and eat with the people,

Dismissal time at Santa Rosa School in Lima, Peru. Sister Alma Bernadette lets the best girl for the day have the privilege of taking home Our Lady's statue overnight.

(Right) *Sister Socorro Maria listens as a young Panamanian tells her the story of the Annunciation.*

(Below) *The children in the Sisters' Panamanian schools often came from families who lived in crowded one-room huts, such as this one in the Chorillo district in the Canal Zone.*

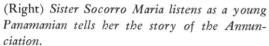

THE LORD IS WITH
AN ANGEL CAME TO MA
IT WAS THE ANGEL OF T

teach them the doctrine, and if there is a Sister-nurse along, care for their medical needs.

The most recent development in Latin America is the Sisters' social-service work. The Maryknoll Sisters have twenty-six qualified social workers practicing their profession in seven mission countries and the United States. The work in the States is centered mainly in San Francisco and Hawaii, where social work is highly organized under both public and private auspices. Such services are very limited in Latin America.

In 1954 Sister Rose Dominic came from the diocesan social-service agency in Honolulu to set up a Social Center in the new Maryknoll parish of Santa Rosa in Lima, Peru. What little social service had been done by the Church in this ancient and beautiful capital city was administered by a few parish social-service centers. There was no diocesan program. Government services were almost negligible. The poor, for the most part, did not know where to turn for help. Compared to Hawaii, which has one of the best integrated social-service programs, Lima was an uncharted ocean.

As a result of Sister Rose Dominic's interest in them, and the services she placed at their disposal, the people of Santa Rosa became acquainted with the idea of coming to the parish social-service center when they needed help. At first they came only in the last desperate crisis. Even of these, there were very many.

From the beginning, Sister Rose Dominic had the wholehearted support of Señorita Rosario Arraoz, who had played a major role in the preliminary steps that led to the establishment of Santa Rosa parish, where she lived. Señorita Arraoz moved into an apartment in order to turn over her home to serve as the Maryknoll Fathers' first rectory and chapel. She had founded the National School of Social Service, and had served as its Director for twenty-six years. It had been her dream to have Maryknoll Sisters develop a strong Catholic Social Service program in Lima.

Eventually, through concentrated effort, Sister Rose Dominic was able to develop a strong parish center, which not only served the poor but also provided supervised fieldwork experience for students from both the National and the Catholic University schools of Social Work. Furthermore, Sister was able to help integrate the existing meager welfare services better to serve those most in need. The unemployed found work, expectant mothers received hospital care, desperately ill children received the medicines they required, and food sent from the United States through Caritas reached the hungry. The people of the parish began to organize their efforts to assist one another and to keep one another's needs in mind. In one year, Sister Rose Dominic's office provided social work assistance to 926 families and 305 individuals.

The Archbishop of Lima decided he wanted this program extended throughout his diocese, and asked Sister to handle the expansion. To help her, three more Maryknoll Sister-social workers have been assigned to Peru. In addition, social work centers have been initiated in Bolivia and Chile, where similar programs are now being put into effect.

THE ORIENT

The focus in the Orient in the fifties was on the refugees. In the summer of 1950 men, women, and children poured into Pusan, Korea, from the North; and at the same time into Hong Kong from the China mainland. While the Korean War raged, and for several years afterward, the Pusan Clinic handled up to 2,000 patients daily. When the fighting stopped, the freedom-seeking people of North Korea still strove to get away from Communism by whatever means possible to them. They were all destitute, seeking work and food. Many, many of them were ill, and came to the Sisters' Clinic for help.

During this time the American Armed Forces

Sister Dolores, a nurse, and third-year medical student Sister Ann Fidelis check the line outside the Pusan Clinic for the most critical cases. Sister Ann Fidelis went to Korea on a three-month study grant from Smith, Kline & French Laboratories.

Every child in this treatment room is critically ill, but as yet the Sisters can give them only out-patient care. They handle even tuberculous meningitis on this basis.

Outside the Pediatrics Department in Pusan, a heartbreaking lineup of desperately ill children and desperately poor parents.

(Right) Refugees poured into Hong Kong from the "Red Paradise," and the Sisters' first effort was to provide food and clothing.

A clinic success story. Sister Lois, a doctor from Glens Falls, New York, beams over her healthy young patient, though his mother can still hardly believe it.

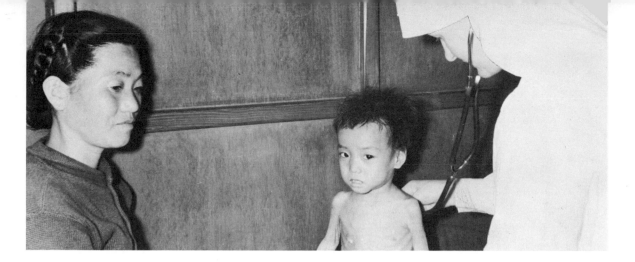

Malnutrition is often the basic ailment that leaves these little ones open to every other disease. Sister Agnus Therese is the doctor.

Audio-Visual aids—Chinese style—help Sister John Andree on Formosa present the Holy Faith to a young mother. The Sisters went to Formosa with many other refugees ousted by the Communists from the mainland of China.

in Korea inaugurated a plan to support the construction of hospitals that could serve the general public in Korean cities. An agreement was reached by which the Maryknoll Sisters would take responsibility for one such hospital in Pusan; and Sister William Marie, a construction technologist, was assigned to cooperate with the Army personnel in supervising the construction. It was to be a long-term job, because of general shortages and the inability to secure or fabricate needed materials.

In the meantime the Sisters' Clinic staff expanded to include five Sister-doctors, seventeen Sister-nurses, and several medical technicians. Korean doctors, nurses, and technicians worked at the Clinic with the Sisters, and the latter often provided on-the-job training for able young Koreans.

Another facet of assistance begun with good success in Korea was the formation of cooperatives. Sister Mary Gabriella studied the cooperative movement in Antigonish, Nova Scotia, and returned to Korea well qualified to begin such groups. She started four, two among the employees of the Clinic and two in parishes near the Clinic.

By 1962 the Maryknoll Sisters had another Clinic in Chung Puk To, were teaching English in two large government high schools in Inchon, and were to open a general hospital in Pusan.

After the bamboo curtain fell, Hong Kong, too, was bulging with refugees. They built themselves shantytowns on the rugged hillsides of the colony, which were periodically wiped out by fire. The Maryknoll Sisters, many of them also refugees from the mainland, inaugurated a plan to build small concrete homes for individual refugee families. Through Mr. Wakefield, the Chief Resettlement Officer, government land was made available to the project. The Sisters campaigned in their own large schools and among Hong Kong businessmen for funds to construct the homes. The refugees themselves did the building, grateful to be working again. In this way hundreds of desti-

Poor children of "Holy Spirit Club" dressed for their parts in "Grandfather's Birthday."

tute people were given a small permanent home.

Later on, as the numbers fleeing Communism grew and grew, the government built "seven-storey mountains"—mammoth tenements housing 2,500 people in each. Although far from ideal, and badly overcrowded, they answered a severe need and provided space for stores and schools. Each area of tenements housed almost 90,000 people. The Sisters began welfare work in several of these areas—Kings Park, Chai Wan, and Tung Tao, Kwan Tong, and Kowloontsai. They opened clinics, day nurseries, and schools. They had as many as 500 adults at a time studying the Faith. The Catholic population of Hong Kong rose from 50,000 to 135,000.

During this time the Sisters' two principal schools—Maryknoll Convent School and Maryknoll Sisters' School—outgrew their premises, and new buildings were constructed to house these institutions. In 1961 the Sisters opened a general hospital, staffed both by their own doctors and by Chinese and European physicians from the Hong Kong colony.

The Sisters also began mission work on Formosa, the last free soil of the Republic of China. Their primary work there is home visiting and instructing converts. They also opened clinics and sent two Sister-doctors, as well as nurses to staff them. A mobile clinic reaches the out-of-the-way mountain villages. The Sisters teach English at two secular universities in Taipei and have a hostel for students attending them. They are also in charge of the formation of a diocesan novitiate. Their missions are at Changhua, Miaoli, Towfen, Poli, Busia, Tahu, Houlung, and Kung Kwan.

HOME FRONT

In the midst of this rehabilitation of missions and expansion to new fields, news came of Mother Mary Joseph's death on October 9, 1955. Mother had suffered a stroke that partially paralyzed her in March, 1952. She was never again able to walk, although she tried, but she did regain some control of her facial muscles and some use of the affected hand. Mother was not of the grit-your-teeth-and-bear-it school of suffering. She believed in relieving suffering when it was medically possible to do so. When it was not possible, God would give His grace to endure it. She strongly held that whatever happened is in some way God's gift. However, she tried to remain active in spite of her paralysis. For example, she went up the hill to see her Cloistered daughters, even though once she had to be transported—wheelchair and all—in the back of a truck.

When news of her death reached the missions—and most of them heard it on the radio that very night—people flocked to the convents to express their sympathy and compassion. Many commented on the Sisters' serenity and peacefulness in the face of such a loss. The Sisters themselves, in all parts of the world, were joy-

fully conscious of Mother's loving presence, as if she had stopped by each mission on her way home to heaven. Many fine eulogies were preached in the far corners of the world, but for her daughters in Christ, the primary consciousness was her resemblance to Christ, when He said: "I am in the midst of you as one who serves." To honor her memory they strove the more to imitate her loving will to serve with an understanding heart.

Mother Mary Columba continued to guide the Community during these years of expansion, having been re-elected for a second term as Mother General in 1952. At the expiration of this second term, the general Chapter which met in 1958 elected Mother Mary Colman the third Mother General of the Congregation.

Although their work in the United States is limited, the Sisters are doing mission work among minority groups in several cities. For instance, the Chinese in New York City had settled largely in Transfiguration parish on Mott Street; Maryknoll Sisters took over the parochial school. A similar school for Chinese was opened in Chicago's Chinatown and a catechetical and welfare center in Boston's. In Los Angeles, a school for Japanese has been in operation for more than forty years, except during the

The Honorable Harry S. Truman was the principal speaker at the dedication of Queen of the World Hospital, Kansas City's first integrated hospital. Shown with Mr. Truman are Mother

Mary Columba, Archbishop Edwin V. O'Hara, who invited the Sisters to staff the hospital, and Sister Mary Mercy, a doctor, who became the hospital's first administrator.

First Communion Day at St. Anthony of Padua in the Bronx, New York. This is one of the very few American parochial schools the Maryknoll Sisters staff.

Sister Christina Marie and an undisturbed infant during an air-raid practice at Transfiguration School in New York City's Chinatown.

Three young Catholic Americans beam their joy at being chosen for the honor of serving at the altar. The Sisters teach in Negro districts of New York and St. Louis.

"Now all we have to do is sort it out and send it to the missions." Sisters Elizabeth Grace and Frederica, nurses at Maryknoll Hospital in Monrovia, California, have their hands full after a successful "Donation Day" campaign.

War. Negroes and Puerto Ricans in parishes in New York, Chicago and St. Louis find the Sisters ready with schools, catechetical and social welfare workers. Mexicans and migrant workers, long neglected in their spiritual needs, are provided with catechists in Stockton and Guadalupe in California, and in Houston, Texas. A parish school attached to the old mission in San Juan Capistrano, California, attracts many Mexican children.

In 1954 the Community accepted the invitation of Archbishop Edwin V. O'Hara to send Maryknoll Sisters to staff an integrated general hospital in Kansas City. Queen of the World Hospital was dedicated in 1955. Of the 140 physicians registered with the hospital, thirty-two are Negroes. The active staff of thirty-five includes fifteen Negroes. In Monrovia, California, the Sisters conduct Maryknoll Hospital, which specializes in chest and lung surgery.

Over New York's WNBC–TV station through an original puppet show called *Let's Talk About God* Sisters also teach Religion.

To make the work and needs of the missions known in the United States, Maryknoll Sisters lecture and show movies to various organizations, in schools and at local and national mission and vocational exhibits.

Tending to the needs of Maryknoll's future priests, as Our Lady cared for the Holy Child, is the work of the Sisters at Mountain View, California and at the Major Seminary at Maryknoll.

The Sisters number several writers and artists in the Community. To mention a few: Sister Juliana has written a number of children's books; with Sister Chaminade, now deceased, she wrote the Sadlier Geographies commonly used in Catholic schools, as well as *Crusade and Treasure Box*. Sister Just, delving into mission history, wrote *Immortal Fire, Rome and Russia, The Glory of Christ* (collaborating with Maryknoll's Father Mark Kent) and *A Digest of Catholic Mission History*. Best known among Maryknoll writers is Sister Maria del Rey whose mission tales in *Pacific Hopscotch, In and Out the Andes, Her Name Is Mercy* and *Dust on My Toes* have made the community's work familiar to thousands of Americans. Her picture-story *Bernie Becomes a Nun* remains a perennial best-seller.

Sister Maria Giovanni's visual aids—sets of pictures and texts on the Life of Our Lord, the Sacraments and other subjects—are in demand by teachers of religion, as are the Chi Rho Arts sculpture and religious cards by Sister Marie Pierre and Sister Marie Francois.

Decked in leis, Mother Mary Columba enjoys some of the schoolchildren at the Kaneohe

Mission with "The Pali" cliff as an awesome backdrop.

Two Filipina beauties on their day of days await serenely God's Greatest Gift.

First Communion Day in the Philippines, and a loving grandmother gives a final touch to a child's veil.

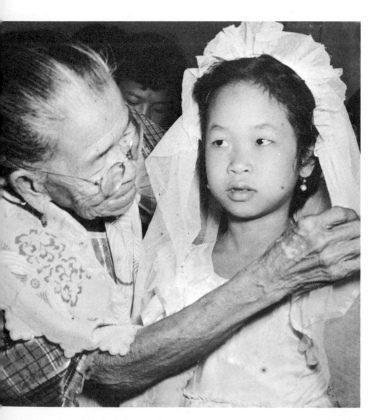

THE PHILIPPINES

Three primary aims underlay the reestablishment and expansion of the Maryknoll Sisters' school system in the Philippines. The Sisters sought to lead souls to God, to train the minds of youth to live fitly here and gain heaven hereafter, and to form lay apostles. By 1961 the Sisters conducted three colleges leading to Liberal Arts and Education degrees, twelve high schools, nine elementary schools, and five kindergartens throughout the Philippines. They also had elementary schools in the Pacific Islands of Yap and Koror. During this time the enrollment in all schools tripled. One high school is in the Moslem territory of Dulawan on Mindanao. Sister-teachers also work in Manila, Quezon City, Malabon, Pakil, Lipa City, Lucena, Baguio, Santiago, Jimenez, Panabo, and Santo Tomas.

Under the direction of Sister Miriam Thomas, who had remained on the Islands as Regional Superior after her release from Los Banos Internment Camp, several buildings were constructed in Quezon City to house Maryknoll College. The college is accredited to give a B.S. in Education in addition to its other Liberal Arts and Science degrees. It is the culmination of the Sisters' system of education by which they strive to develop wholeness and holiness in their pupils. Approximately 30 per cent of the college students are studying on scholarships, without which they could not continue their education. The college students have an opportunity to work toward an Archdiocesan diploma qualifying them to teach Religion in the schools and colleges throughout the Islands.

The other main work in the Philippines is catechetics. Many of the catechists are volunteers from among the Sisters' students and from among the employees at the hospital at Manapla. To help train catechists, the Sisters conduct Catechetical Institutes at several of their schools during the summer months. The first such Institute, held at Lipa, attracted sixty young people, including twelve seminarians. The following year one hundred took the course. When the

At Pakil, the Philippines, the people are fisher-folk. This is one of the many towns in which the Sisters concentrate on high-school education, to focus their pupils toward a full spiritual, professional, and social life. Sister Miriam Emmanuel inspects her pupil's catch.

Praying to St. Thomas Kosaki, boy martyr, reminds these children that Japan has a long and glorious list of martyrs for the Faith.

press of work prevented the Sisters at Lucena from continuing such an Institute, two graduates of Maryknoll College volunteered to take over the program under the direction of their pastor.

That the Sisters are achieving their aims is attested to in a letter from Attorney Jeremias Montemayor, Dean of Ateneo University Law School, and Founder and President of the Federation of Free Farmers. He wrote:

DEAR SISTERS:

I would like to write you on something which has been on my mind for some time now. We have two daughters in your grade school, and relatives in other of your schools. We would like you to know that the education you give our daughters has always been a source of consolation, joy and wonder to us.

We think that you give the best type of education for Filipina girls. It seems the reason is that you are able to supply their deficiencies and to enhance their good qualities. Filipina girls are often extremely shy and reserved, which sometimes appears like languor or even rudeness. You help them overcome this defect by instilling self-confidence, self-possession, and a sense of the joy of living. Any danger of their being led to sophistication or even looseness, is prevented by the spirit of holiness and modesty which you inspire in them. Much of this, I think, comes from the best traits of the American character, which is so full of vitality, enthusiasm, outspokenness and simplicity.

My wife and I would also like to express our appreciation and gratitude to you and all for being what you are. We believe that this is actually the most effective way by which you are educating our children. You radiate a spirit of holiness and purity which does not in any way lessen your humanity. You appear to us as always happy, always full of vitality and most near to God, and hence, most near to God's children and God's world.

Personally, you often make it easy for me to think of Our Blessed Mother. We certainly are fortunate to have you around to help prepare our children to be good children of Our Lord.

Sincerely yours in Christ,

/s/ JEREMIAS MONTEMAYER

JAPAN 1950–1962

In Japan, Catechetics is the main work of the Sisters. They also teach English to students of all ages, and immediately after the classes they give doctrine instruction for which many of their pupils remain.

Sister Gloria established Mission Arts, which provides employment for twenty women making vestments. They are given an opportunity to study the Faith, and many do. Converts among these women are outstanding in the example they give in good Christian marriages; several have received the gift of a religious vocation. Sister extended this work also to women who cannot leave their homes, and forty young mothers are thus employed.

There are today only 300,000 Catholics among Japan's 90,000,000, but now, as through the centuries, the quality of their Faith is remarkable. Japan boasts twenty-six canonized saints, two hundred called Blessed, and numberless martyrs. In Urakami, Nagasaki, and the Goto Islands, bands of Christians kept the Faith through centuries of persecution without priests or Sacraments except Baptism and Matrimony. When missioners were again allowed into Japan, these Faithful were discovered, and March 17th is celebrated on the Church calendar in Japan as "Finding of the Christians" day.

The Maryknoll Sisters work in the Buddhist center Kyoto, and the Shinto stronghold Ise. They also began mission work at Tsu, Hikone, Otsu, Sai-in, Takano, Ueno, Kujo, and in 1959 went to the northern island of Hokkaido to begin mission work at Muroran and later Tomákamai.

The May crowning ends in a blaze of glory. Candles symbolize Faith the world over.

They began retreat days for women at the Kyoto Center house, and ordinarily sixty attend. On August 15th the Japanese honor their dead and invite them to revisit their homes. On that day the Sisters emphasize the Christian significance of the departure of Our Lady for heaven by having a living rosary, tableaux of the Christian mysteries, and a candlelight procession to an outdoor shrine. They introduce parishioners to such varied activities as scouting and the Legion of Mary. It was a minor miracle to get the gentle, self-effacing Japanese women to do house-to-house visiting and to approach strangers in hospitals and other institutions. Nevertheless in ten years the Kyoto Diocese had forty-six presidia of the Legion, through whose work many found the Faith and Catholicism flourished.

CEYLON

Only in Ceylon was the good work of God brought to an abrupt end. The government, which in 1948 had invited the Maryknoll Sisters to staff a hospital in Kandy, in 1959 found excuses to debar them—and all other Religious—from such charitable work. When the Sisters were removed from the Civil Hospital in Kandy, Catholics and others in Ceylon were indignant at such insincerity toward them.

One paper stated: "The Cabinet decided that every nun in government service should be served with marching orders as soon as it could be conveniently managed . . . the Government resolved to purge the Island's nursing service of some of its most efficient and devoted personnel. But because suitable qualified Ceylonese substitutes could not be easily produced or spared and because the nuns, owing to their dedication and efficiency, were popular with Tamil and Singalese, Buddhist, Hindu, Muslim and Christian patients alike, the process of their expulsion was planned to be unobtrusively piecemeal."

In 1959 ten Sisters left Ceylon for other mission fields. The remaining Sisters opened a clinic

Sister Michael Francis dispenses a bit of Tender Loving Care as prescribed, at Civil Hospital, Kandy, Ceylon.

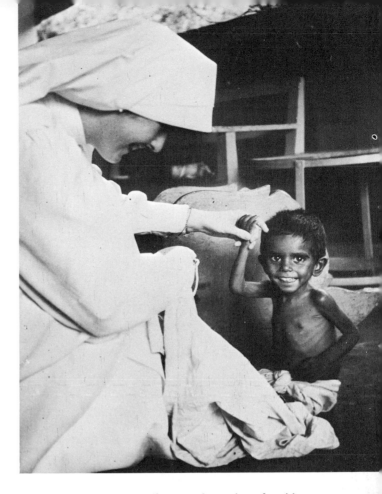

It may be his first smile for a long time, but it's worth working for, isn't it? Ceylon children and Sister Michael Francis were "naturals."

and maternity ward for the workers of a plantation outside the city, in Padiwatte. However, pressure of circumstances forced them to discontinue this work and to leave Ceylon in March, 1962.

MISSION AIMS

The training of a missionary Sister is not a simple matter. The individual's wholehearted response to God's call is only the first step toward becoming a Maryknoll Sister. Her specific spiritual formation begins when she enters the postulancy. Nor is it a nebulous ideal; it is a definite and spiritual reality taught and experienced in an atmosphere of loving holiness. This development is sharply focused in the novitiate, but it grows in depth and wholeness throughout the life of a Religious.

In keeping with the counsel of Pope Pius XII in his Encyclical "On Promoting Catholic Missions," she should have not only the spiritual training that befits her as a Religious but should learn in addition those subjects that will be most useful in her mission work—languages, medicine, teaching techniques, and social work. Whatever her field, a mission Sister's holiness and relation to God are enhanced by a competence in her specific work through which it may be expressed to others. God has generously given Maryknoll fine vocations, and the Community has accepted the responsibility of developing its members wholly to serve others. This training is lengthy, expensive, and thorough, but it puts a best foot forward for the Church and America.

Elizabeth Makra entered the postulancy at Maryknoll in October, 1926. She was a graduate of Ursuline Academy in Cleveland. After her religious profession as Sister Mary Lelia, she graduated with a B.A. from Mount St. Vincent's College in New York. She was assigned to Manchuria, where she studied Mandarin and began teaching in this language in 1935. After being interned and repatriated during World War II,

Bishop Fulton Sheen and Mother Mary Columba at the Motherhouse in 1952.

Mother Mary Colman was elected Mother General in 1958. She had spent sixteen years in the Philippines and knew much of the mission world at firsthand.

Sister Lelia went to Panama for three years. Subsequently she returned to the States and attended Catholic University in Washington, D.C., where she earned her M.A. in Oriental (Mandarin) Language and Culture. She was reassigned to the work with the Chinese in Hong Kong for ten years. In 1961 Sister Lelia's translation of the *Hsiao Ching*, a Chinese classic on filial piety, was published by St. John's University Press, Brooklyn.

In 1939 Doris Higgins, a graduate of Sacred Heart High School, Yonkers, New York, joined Maryknoll. After graduating from Maryknoll Teachers College, as Sister Joan Muriel, she was assigned to the Canal Zone. Here Sister became acutely aware of the need of catechetical training to teach the Faith to others, and even more to train catechists. She returned to the States in 1955 and began studying the Confraternity of Christian Doctrine methods. Finally she went to Catholic University, Washington, D.C., and took the Confraternity's leadership training course. Sister was then reassigned to Chile,

(Above) *More than a hundred young girls each year decide they want to be Maryknoll Sisters. They come from all parts of the United States and from foreign countries as well.*

Sister Rose Thaddeus smiles, not in anticipation of a good meal, but because she finds happiness in working out her vocation.

In union there is strength. Learning to pray together the Divine Office, the official prayer of the Church, forges a bond of unity.

where she has organized a catechists' school to train leaders in towns and villages to teach the doctrine to their neighbors.

Mary Hotz of Delphos, Ohio, entered Maryknoll in 1946. She was a high-school graduate. After her religious profession in 1949, Sister David Ann was assigned to study at Maryknoll Teachers College. She earned her B.S. in Education and went on to St. Louis University, where she was awarded a Master's Degree in Social Work. Sister is now doing social work at the diocesan bureau in Hawaii.

In 1946 Veronica Klus of Wisconsin and Chicago entered Maryknoll after graduation from high school. She too went through the customary three years of postulancy and novitiate. In 1949 she was professed Sister Ann Veronica, and began her studies at Maryknoll Teachers College. She continued at Manhattanville, now at Purchase, New York, where she earned her B.A., with concentration on premedical subjects. She went on to Marquette University in Milwaukee, and in 1956 earned her M.D. After her internship at St. Mary's in Rochester, New

Visitors comment on the grounds at Maryknoll, but there is much work that goes into them. Raking leaves and garden work serves a double purpose: they give the Sisters outdoor exercise and provide beauty spots to enjoy.

York, and training in surgery at St. Vincent's in New York City, Sister Ann Veronica was assigned to the missions in Korea. She is on the staff of the Pusan Clinic and will be one of four Sister-doctors on the staff of the Maryknoll Sisters Armed Forces Memorial Hospital when it opens.

These are examples of the training given Maryknoll Sisters, whose work is to bring the good news of God's Love to the world. The whole program of services rendered by Maryknoll Sisters is basically social welfare. Going to serve people of another race or nationality, they aim to study and absorb their culture, to learn their language, to become one of them, to discover and to foster their natural strengths and resources, to help them meet their social needs, and above all to help them to recognize their own personal dignity as children of God. The formation of a Maryknoll Sister is geared to approach this task with respect and reverence for the people served, with a delicate regard for their rules of etiquette, and with genuine humility.

The great upsurge of social-welfare programs currently undertaken by governmental and voluntary agencies under the leadership of the United Nations, reaching vast areas and unprecedented numbers, is justifiably attracting worldwide attention. Both Pope Pius XII and Pope John XXIII have urged that Catholics give these programs the fullest cooperation.

Social workers who have served where Western culture has not penetrated report that one

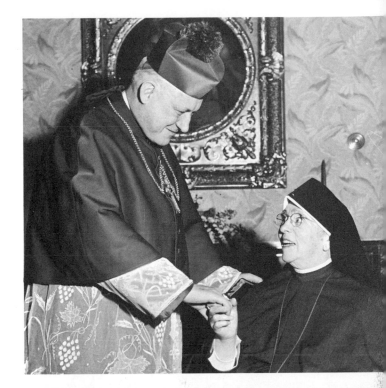

Cardinal Cushing and Mother Mary Joseph were constant friends. (Above) They exchange a handclasp at the dedication of Ladycrest, Maryknoll Novitiate at Topsfield, Massachusetts. This was the Cardinal's gift to the Sisters. (Below) The altar in the new chapel at Ladycrest is modern and world-minded.

Novices pronounce in a clear voice the vows of poverty, chastity, and obedience. Seated here is Father Anthony Cotta, the Sister's chaplain for more than thirty years, who took many of the early-day pictures in this book.

Sister Maria Pastores, her studies completed at
Maryknoll Teachers' College, is ready for her
mission assignment to Japan.

of their greatest surprises is to find absence of respect for the dignity of the human personality. Similarly, students who come here from such countries comment that it is for them a new concept.

This dignity of the human personality and the resulting awareness of the need to serve others less privileged is historically derived from Judeo-Christian tradition.

Going out to other races to bring them the message of Christ, the Sisters usually begin by meeting the needs of the distressed, underprivileged, discouraged people. This service to others regardless of race or creed is performed as an expression of Christian charity. Service selflessly given is often a new experience for these people who seek to learn the motivation behind it. This may in turn lead to a study of the Faith that provides the motivation. This can open up a new way of life rooted in love, in contrast to what has often been one of fear or hate. This new way of life brings a new approach to meeting social problems, through learning how to put into practice the principles of Christian social living.

The services rendered by the Maryknoll Sisters as teachers, doctors, nurses, and social workers are thus, first of all, a loving expression of their own spirit of charity and also a frequent means of attracting people to the Faith they would like to share with all the world.

At this point it might be well to point out that the particular pattern the Maryknoll Sisters' program takes in any given area is determined in general by local needs and more specifically by the Bishop of the diocese and the priests with whom the Sisters are associated.

The Sisters maintain hospitals, clinics, schools, and colleges of their own. In Africa, the Orient, Hawaii, Latin America, and in the States they work with the Maryknoll Fathers; in Hawaii with the Sacred Hearts Fathers; in Nicaragua with the Capuchins; in Panama with the Vincentians; in the Marshall and Caroline Islands with the Jesuits; and in the Orient with the Oblates of Mary Immaculate, the La Salette Fathers, and the Columbans.

Fitting into the general program of the Catholic Church in the given area, the Sisters naturally concentrate on works that will reach the women and children. While general medical services will naturally be available to men as well as to women, the Sisters are always specially interested in promoting infant welfare through clinics, classes, and midwifery training, and using these contacts as a stepping-stone to fostering Christian social living in homes.

In addition to whatever professional services they undertake, Maryknoll Sisters lay great stress on the value of person-to-person contact, and always include carefully planned home visiting as part of their program. Used as a means of making friends in the beginning, home visiting always remains an important part of the work.

Like all Catholic missioners, the Maryknoll Sisters go to another race or people primarily to bring to them a knowledge of Christ. Belief in Christ's teaching necessarily involves adopting the Christian way of life. This brings about a slow process of transformation, both in ideas and in the daily business of living, by which the Sisters seek slowly but surely to effect a materially better and a spiritually higher level of social living. The Maryknoll Sisters have received abundantly of the graciousness of God; of the high ideals of Christ; of the concrete generosity of Americans. From this treasure these American missioners seek to bring forth new things and old.

(Above) *Sister Joel in the chemistry laboratory at Maryknoll Teachers' College at the Motherhouse.*

(Below) *The Sisters turn their hands to just about everything. For instance, many are good at photographic darkroom work.*

Music, biology, and foreign languages are all part of the student's life as she studies at Maryknoll Teachers' College. Tapes are available for Chinese, Tagalog, Kiswahili, and Japanese, as well as for French and Spanish lessons.

(Below) *Gruffy, Trilly, and the Maryknoll Sisters have taught religion over WNBC-TV in New York for more than four years every Sunday. Here is Happy Cap, too, a monkey who makes things lively at times. Sister Serra, who started them off on a TV career, is now at Morogoro, Africa.*

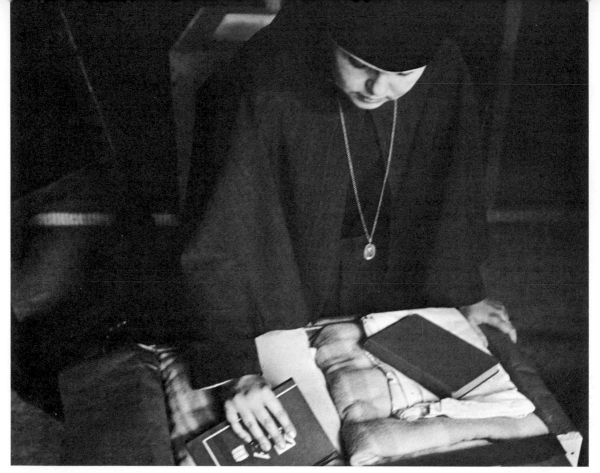

Once assigned to a foreign mission, Sisters must pack their equipment and supplies to be used for various professions in primitive places. Because there is usually no hope of replacing anything if it is broken, things are packed with care.

A-22   37 X 21 X 16
        CU FT. 7.2

MARYKNOLL SISTERS
& EXPESS TRANSPORT CO.
MOMBASA - KENYA
BRITISH EAST AFRICA

About fifty Sisters each year leave on ships and planes for scattered parts of the world. The Maryknoll habit is familiar on ocean paths and the skyways of the globe.

ACKNOWLEDGMENTS

ALL PHOTOGRAPHS are the property of the Mary-knoll Sisters except for the following: frontispiece courtesy Bachrach; page 110 and page 170 (bottom) courtesy United Press International; page 119 (bottom), page 164 (top), page 166 (top and bottom), page 169, and page 174 (bottom) courtesy *Look* magazine; page 126 (bottom) courtesy Martha Holmes for *Time* magazine; and page 165 courtesy George W. Barris.

GREENLAND

ALASKA

CANADA

ICELAND

UNITED

STATES

GREAT
BRITAIN

FRAN

$\mathcal{A}\mathcal{T}\mathcal{L}\mathcal{A}\mathcal{N}\mathcal{T}\mathcal{I}\mathcal{C}$

$\mathcal{O}\mathcal{C}\mathcal{E}\mathcal{A}\mathcal{N}$

PORTUGAL

SPAIN

MOROCCO

ALGER

MEXICO

SP.SAHARA

HAWAII

CUBA

PUERTO
RICO

MAURITANIA

MALI

GUATEMALA

NICARAGUA

SENEGAL

PANAMA

VENEZUELA

GUINEA

COLOMBIA

LIBERIA

$\mathcal{P}\mathcal{A}\mathcal{C}\mathcal{I}\mathcal{F}\mathcal{I}\mathcal{C}$

ECUADOR

EQUATOR

GHANA

GA

PERU

BRAZIL

$\mathcal{O}\mathcal{C}\mathcal{E}\mathcal{A}\mathcal{N}$

BOLIVIA

PARAGUAY

CHILE

ARGENTINA

URUGUAY

Countries with Maryknoll establishments